Urban Social Areas

BRIAN T. ROBSON

Theory and Practice in Geography

OXFORD UNIVERSITY PRESS · 1975

Oxford University Press, Ely House, London W. 1

GLASGOW NEW YORK TORONTO MELBOURNE WELLINGTON
CAPE TOWN IBADAN NAIROBI DAR ES SALAAM LUSAKA ADDIS ABABA
DELHI BOMBAY CALCUTTA MADRAS KARACHI LAHORE DACCA
KUALA LUMPUR SINGAPORE HONG KONG TOKYO

ISBN 0 19 874036 0

© Oxford University Press 1975

Printed in Great Britain
by J. W. Arrowsmith Ltd., Bristol

Contents

Introduction

'The urban crisis', 'the housing problem', 'the failure of planning', 'the poverty trap', 'planning blight'—all are common terms in current parlar Even 'suburbia', once heralded as the solution to the ills of high-density urban life, is a term now used more often in disapprobation than in est Cities, in short, seem in a mess. Why can we not understand cities and why can we not control and manipulate them to produce fewer crises and less evident injustice amongst urban population? Their complexity is one obvious answer. Attempted solutions to one problem have wide ramifications and may often have effects of an unexpected and wholly undesirable kind elsewhere. Generations of reformers have eagerly clear the warrens and hovels of urban slums only to find the displaced population resurface in newly-created slums which re-create the conditions from which households had been cleared. Betterment taxes, which aim to secure the benefit of rising land values for society rather than private individuals, have led to shortages of available land.

The contribution to our understanding of cities which has been mad by academics, and by academic geography in particular, has been of son substance, but has certainly not led to any notable improvement in the formulation of plans or of policy. To some extent this is because of the curious fossilization of urban theory. Cities have changed in response to changes in technology, changes in production and distribution within th economy, and changes in the social structure of the population, but urb theory has changed little to keep abreast. The 'Victorian' industrial city is still much to the forefront in urban geography, and, at the back of ou minds, the ideal type is still a romanticized view of Chicago, the city which, for the urban geographer, has become the seed bed of theory, th norm, the point of reference, the source of urban fact and urban fiction

Two points, related to this fossilization, need to be made at the outse of this book. First, it is important to remember that cities in the develo world are not separate, readily-identifiable objects which can be abstrac from the remainder of society. The increase in long-distance commuting and in general physical mobility has made it ever more difficult to draw realistic boundaries around cities, but the implications are wider than this methodological quibble. The demands for housing and for the whol array of urban amenities in a town can no longer be calculated in terms of the households who live or work within its administrative bounds, an this has obvious consequences for plans for the provision of urban facili for the financial basis of such provision, and for the costs and benefits o what is built and provided. Consider some of the difficulties: where urba commuters look for permanent or for second homes in rural areas, the cost of housing is forced up beyond the levels which local households can afford; where a local authority makes provision for the homeless, the greater mobility of households makes it likely that the problem of homelessness in that area will increase as families are attracted to it, as certain London boroughs have found; where an area attracts households without any parallel industry or commerce, its local tax base might be denuded. Such difficulties arise partly from the increasing overlap and interdigitation of what we still tend to think of as separate, identifiable cities. Cities, in fact, have become increasingly synonymous with society.

Second, in looking at any general urban theories or models we must bear in mind the particular effects of cultural differences between different societies. The early writings from Chicago were notoriously parochial in this respect, and it was with some consternation that patterns very different from Chicago were later found in the cities of Latin America and Europe. This same cultural myopia seems a danger today in the suggestion, for example, of a universal three-factor model of urban residential structure (Berry, 1965). Studies in countries outside the United States have shown the importance of cultural differences (Abu-Lughod, 1969; Landay, 1971) and have revived the long-standing debate about the cultural impress upon 'natural' processes (by which is often meant commercial-industrial economies guided by a capitalist system) which create the form of cities. Berry (1973) has recently written an impressive survey of world urbanization which he tellingly subtitles 'divergent paths in the urban experience of the twentieth century', and in which he stresses the differential effects of the varying degrees of central control in the economies of North American, European, and developing countries. A frequently quoted example which underlines his point is Musil's (1968) study of Prague, in which, after the development of a centrally directed communist regime, residential differentiation in the town declined markedly. Since rents are now heavily subsidized and housing is allocated in terms of need rather than of ability-to-pay, the correlation of house size with household income has declined and there is, instead, a greater association between family size and age on the one hand, the house size and price on the other. Too much can, of course, be made of such differences, since the 'hidden hand' of capital and of competition can manifest itself in various ways. Even in a communist regime, for example, the legacy of the past lies heavy on the decisions of the present. In Yugoslavian towns, even though land has been taken into central control and differential land values have ostensibly been abolished, the greater density of housing in the central areas means that the costs of demolition and rebuilding are higher than in peripheral areas since more households have to be rehoused (Winnick, 1966). Legislation and other cultural characteristics of a society never the less play a vital part in determining the form of cities and the nature of the social areas within them.

6 Urban social areas

Since much of the urban theory is American in origin, it is interesting to point briefly to some crude differences between the United States and Britain which might affect the nature of cities in the two areas. First, the size and significance of minority groups is very different. Second, most of the towns in Britain are much older, and the tangible legacy of earlier life-styles and economic and social structures embedded in the physical inheritance of British towns is the more telling. Third, the political organization of local authorities differs; the semi-autonomous suburban authorities which girdle most large American cities have exacerbated the problem of providing services in central cities whose tax bases have been more radically eroded than in Britain, where less finance is derived locally, and where, especially after the reorganization of local government in 1974, boundaries have encompassed more all-inclusive central and peripheral areas. The problems have been different in degree if not in kind. Fourth, the differences in the overall degree of central control in the two countries have had effect in numerous ways. One of the most dramatic is the provision of state-subsidized housing which in America began only in 1937 and now provides a mere 3 per cent of total housing (Fuerst, 1974), whereas in Britain it began in 1919 and now provides 31 per cent of the houses. The postwar development of the planning machine in Britain, allied with the country's smaller size and consequent shortage of land, has also led to a more determined containment of urban sprawl and to the perpetuation of higher densities than typically characterize the development of American towns. The reconstruction of central cities damaged in the war, and (with the capital and expertise thus generated) the rebuilding of other city centres more recently, has involved the investment of large capital sums in the central parts of British cities, and, with the underpinning of the planning philosophy of urban containment, this has helped to delay or defer the erosion of the commercial dominance of urban cores in Britain and, unlike America, has put a more effective damper on the large-scale development of out-of-town shopping centres.

Again, such differences should be seen in proportion (Clawson and Hall, 1973), but cultural differences are important and warrant more than a passing footnote. The great bulk of urban research has been concerned with American cities and it is inevitable that many of the references and examples drawn upon here should be from that work. Whenever possible, however, studies of British towns will be cited, not out of misplaced chauvinism, but to take account of the differences in the British housing market, social structure, legislation, and planning.

Living in towns

Our substantive interest in the social areas of towns stems from the evident fact that social characteristics are very unevenly distributed in space. Why is the geographer interested in this and what conclusions does

he draw from it? First, the fact of social similarities between residents of
a particular part of a town reveals something of how cities 'function', of
how demand and supply intersect in space in the urban housing market.
There are also practical implications stemming from this. A knowledge of
the social geography of a city helps in planning its present and future
needs; the location of welfare services, the areas in greatest need of
housing assistance, the areas likely to 'produce' social problems. Second,
either explicitly or implicitly, the geographer may argue that the homo-
geneity of social areas has social significance in a more direct fashion;
that the area of manual households provides a very different environment,
both physically and socially, from that of white-collar households, and
that two households with otherwise identical characteristics would be
different 'objects' if one lived in the first and the other in the second
type of area. A manual household may therefore differ if it lives in
Bethnal Green or in Woodford (Willmott and Young, 1960). If a manual
household is surrounded by similar families all of whom are likely to have
a 'manual' reference group its ambitions, beliefs, *mores,* and behaviour
may well be reinforced. If however, a manual household is in closer proximity to and more aware of the ideas and life-style of non-manual households, it may be encouraged to change its reference group; it may be
impelled either into a greater individual ambition or into a more conscious
withdrawal and demonstration of its differences.

The place where a household lives may therefore be seen to *reflect*
and to *affect* its social attributes. Location *reflects* social characteristics
in that, within such constraints as its income, a household chooses housing and chooses an area so as to give spatial expression to its image of its
own social standing. Where we find exceptions to the general rule of occupational segregation the location of a 'deviant' household can often be
explained by its history of social mobility—the downwardly-mobile household frequently being found in areas of 'higher' social status. Location
may also *affect* social characteristics, although this is more difficult to
substantiate or to refute. Studies which have tried to establish the relationship have often looked at rather exceptional or extreme situations.
Festinger's (1950) classic study of the effect of distance on friendship
patterns is an example, since he studied the very artificial context of a
student housing complex: families in blocks of flats showed a striking
pattern of acquaintances which was determined by the micro-ecology of
the distances between front doors and the placing of staircases; families
in cul-de-sacs showed a similar influence of distance. Kuper's (1953)
study in Coventry provides a parallel case. Given both the unusual homo-
geneity of the households involved and the fact that the 'communities'
were instantaneously created, the closest parallel in 'normal' residential
areas is the early period in the establishment of a housing estate when the
initial residents face common difficulties and in which, during this 'learn-
ing' stage, the ties between immediate neighbours are often very strong.

Over time, however, distance itself plays a subordinate role and people select friends on the basis of common interests rather than mere proximity, so that residents' associations formed in the early years of an estate usually wither rapidly (Durant, 1939; Morris and Mogey, 1965). The same argument about distance also underlies studies of marriage choices which consistently show that there is a rapid fall-off in marriage partners as the distance between their two pre-marriage locations increases. Cities are socially segregated so that, for a socially endogamous marriage, the number of potential marriage partners is likely to be less at greater distances, but, even where the social and distance aspects are held constant, both have been shown to play a significant and independent role (Ramsøy, 1966).

The role of location in reflecting or affecting social attributes is often merely implied rather than demonstrated in geographical studies. Many sociologists are unimpressed by the assumption that geographical patterns have any social significance, Dennis (1958), for example, suggests:

People seem to find it extraordinarily difficult to realise that mere living together in the same locality can result in a conglomeration of very little sociological importance. The difficulty is immeasurably increased, apparently, when the people in the locality are socially homogeneous; and yet clearly, more than mere aggregation is needed to make a group, however homogeneous the aggregation may be.

Such dissatisfaction with a purely ecological approach to social areas has prompted more socially based definitions of 'community', but the term is infuriatingly nebulous; Hillery (1955), for example, looks at no fewer than 94 definitions. We can, however, concentrate on two aspects of a community: the existence of social contact between its members, and the sense of common social purpose shared by them. We can also recognize two very general types of community which, although they overlap in many contexts, can usefully be thought of as distinct.

Locality-based social systems

In the locality-based community the area in which people live is itself an important component of the sense of community. Contacts are predominantly between people living within the area, and they embrace the whole range of an individual's social activities. Neighbours and kin act as an ever-present matrix—mothers help at the birth of their daughters' children, neighbours are on hand in emergencies, contacts are casually made in the street. Bethnal Green, prototype of such areas, was a happy hunting ground for sociologists in the 1950s, but studies of other such 'working-class' areas include those of St Ebbe's in Oxford (Mogey, 1956) and St Ann's in Nottingham (Coates and Silburn, 1970). It is in such areas that one might look for the traditional picture of a communal 'working-class' world; a common adherence to local group values, the notion of an 'us/them' dichotomy, an evaluation of people 'in the round' an inhibition of individual ambition. That such communities are so in-variably seen in areas of manual households reflects the idea that the manual worker's geographical mobility is lower and that his horizons are more limited by the constraints of distance (Fried and Gleicher, 1961). In the white-collar suburb the density of social contacts may be just as great, but their nature is seen as different: they transcend the local area, being fostered by national media and able to survive transplanation from one suburb to another; they are more formal, more instrumental, more focused on specific aspects of the households' lives.

Whether such locality-based and all-embracing communities exist today (or indeed ever did exist in the extreme form in which they are often painted) is open to debate. The street parties which celebrated the Coronation in the 1950s seem a far cry from the World Cup viewed pri-vately on the colour televisions of households in the 1970s. Increasing affluence, the widening of social horizons and the possible changes in reference groups which this implies, may or may not have destroyed the basis of 'communal' working-class life. Certainly the destruction of long-standing areas through urban renewal has done much to shake loose the chains of social contacts forged through long association in a common geographical area, and has eroded the stability needed for the persistence of dense networks of social contact. Whether such renewal and relocation of households fundamentally uproots and permanently destroys this traditional form of local community is doubtful. It was one of the tenets of the writings of the 1950s and 1960s that it did, but Willmott's (1963) study of Dagenham suggested to the contrary that, over time, the social patterns re-appear, albeit in modified form; people still contacted their kin, and the family-based nuclear household had not entirely displaced the 'extended', more locality-based household of the traditional pattern.

Where such locality-based communities exist, the socially homogeneous geographical social areas and the interaction-based communities obviously overlap, but one must nevertheless accept the importance of a hierarchical array of 'communities' at different scales. Numerous studies show that people recognize different levels of attachment of an area—the set of neighbouring houses, the street, the collection of adjacent streets, the whole town. It is perhaps only at the very smallest scale that one can validly think of an area-based community, and, even here, social contacts may depend very much on the age of the households concerned, since dependence on the local area varies markedly with age. Small children and mothers with young families are more tied to and dependent upon their local area than are older children; the elderly are similarly restricted. Such varying spatial scales and the different levels of physical mobility make it extremely difficult to draw precise spatial boundaries even to the locality-based community since one is still dealing with a relative concept—the relative density of overlapping sets of social relationships.

Common-interest social groups

The community of common interest is comprised of people linked by more specific ties. Common interests may be formed around a wide variety of foci—child rearing, politics, sport, religion—and many of the shared interests, being specific, are likely to be expressed through formal rather than informal associations. The study of such ties obviously requires more than the mere tabulation of the social characteristics of households in an area. It calls for the analysis of social networks, contact patterns, and life-styles of individuals in the form of sociometric studies, well illustrated at a small scale by Whyte's (1943) study of a street gang or, at a larger scale, Stacey's (1960) study of Banbury which looks at the cross-cutting allegiances of individuals in the fields of politics, religion, recreation, and work, and highlights the cleavages between long-established residents and newcomers to the town—a distinction which appears in innumerable studies of commuting and suburban situations.

A frequent type of common interest is that which is produced by some form of external threat which gives rise to a community which is forged by a common defensive interest and at the same time is often centred on a distinct locality. Such communities can be thought of as being based on conflict and may either by short-lived, as in the case of groups formed in opposition to the threat of urban renewal (Dennis, 1972), or longer-lived, as in the conflict communities based on religious or ethnic differences (Boal, 1972).

Studies of community structure and of social life in towns suggest, first, that the nuclear family and house-based activities have grown increasingly important over time and, second, that distance constraints have weakened so that the local area has become increasingly less important. In the age of television, home ownership, and do-it-yourself, both the manual and non-manual workers increasingly concentrate their social activities in the home and this is exacerbated by the growing tendency for husbands and wives to share the tasks of home-centred life, to form what Young and Willmott (1973) call the 'symmetrical family'. The difference between manual and non-manual households becomes, not the traditional distinction between communal and individualistic, but the difference between the extent to which they join more formal associations outside the home, in which it is the non-manual household which continues to play a substantially greater part. The decline of distance constraints has led, at the same time, to less spatially determined communities. The lexicographically fertile Webber (1963; 1964) talks of 'community without propinquity' and of 'urban places and non-place urban realms' in which the ties of common interest transcend the shackles of space so that the spatial bonds of community have been shattered. But, paradoxically, at a very small scale, local ties do persist. The commuters from peripheral villages form associations at the very local level at the same time as they are tied in to social networks and interest groups whose other members may be very far-flung geographically. At a local level the commuter may sit on the parish council, attend meetings of the local parent-teachers association, form a group to defend the elm trees on the village common. But at the same time, he may work in an office in the centre of a distant large town, his wife may teach in a comprehensive school within that same town and attend pottery classes in extra mural courses held in another village, they will both entertain their work colleagues who live in entirely different villages, spend occasional week-ends visiting old friends who live elsewhere in Britain, telephone their parents who live over 100 miles away, visit them at public holidays, and leave their children with them when they take a second holiday at Easter. The far-flung contacts at one level are complemented by a network of other and more local ties.

Divisions in society

It is one of the ironies of the workings of present-day urban society that, in the midst of growing affluence and of the convergence of the 'lower' white-collar and 'upper' black-collar households, the operation of the mixed economy of Britain tends to broaden the gap between poor households and the remainder of the population. The polarity has a strong geographical component, with the poor and very poor segregated in housing terms in the rented housing market and segregated in physical terms in the centres of large cities. The poverty trap is one structural mechanism by which such polarity is maintained and intensified. The fact that welfare 'payments' are linked to a household's financial resources means that if earnings rise, welfare benefits fall. Changes in the distribution of employment opportunities and the operation of the housing market tend also to pull apart employment and housing opportunities and help to concentrate impoverished households in city centres. The central areas of large cities may be in process of becoming sink holes in which deprivation and poverty catch households in an inexorable downward spiral. This is very evident in geographical studies of social *malaise* which consistently show marked contrasts between inner and outer areas of towns. Areas of economic and social *malaise* are coincident and the symptoms are frequently found in central areas—poor schooling, inadequate and insecure housing, low wages, and the concomitant social indicators of ill-health, crime, and social breakdown. The variety of such evidence is legion. In education, the patterns of low achievement, which have widely been shown to be geographically concentrated, need to be seen against a background of environmental deprivation (Douglas, 1964). The recommendations of the Plowden report of 1967, which advocated the delimitation of 'educational priority areas', gave official recognition to this. Likewise, geographical studies of crime show similar patterns. So do studies of ill-health, in which field the connections with environment can most clearly be established. To quote one example, Giggs's (1970) study of mental disturbance and crime in Barry shows complex patterns of associations with environmental

conditions, but, consistently, central areas have high rates of disorganiz-
ation. Similarly, the distribution of schizophrenia in Nottingham shows
a continuing concentration of high rates in central areas (Giggs, 1973).

Such studies of the distribution of social *malaise* and deprivation all
suffer from their inability to establish conclusively any causal connection
between environmental and social characteristics in the absence of case
studies of individuals or of individual households. Ecological studies
show only the spatial coincidence of variables and such associations cannot demonstrate causal links nor can they apply directly to individuals
living within the areas studied. The first point suggests that, although
schizophrenics, for example, may be found in central areas and in poor
housing, the aetiology of schizophrenia may nevertheless derive from
other causes and schizophrenics may simply gravitate to poor houses.
The second point broaches the partly related question of the 'ecological
fallacy'; the incorrectness of drawing inferences about individuals on the
basis of correlations which apply to statistics drawn from areas. Spatial
data may show, for example, that immigrants live in areas of high crime
rates: in one enumeration district of 1000 households, 400 may be
coloured and 200 may have criminal records. But the aggregated statistics
cannot tell us whether all 200 criminal households are black, all are white,
or whether they are divided in some proportion between the two. All we
know are the marginal cell frequencies for any one area, and similar
marginal frequencies may be derived from innumerable permutations of
internal cell frequencies (Robinson, 1950).

Whether the concentrations of deprivation and *malaise* are or are not
affected by the environment, gross disparities remain between central
and peripheral areas in towns and such disparities seem not to be decreas-
ing in our large towns. The urban economy which produces deep freezes,
colour televisions, double garages, and commuter villages, also produces,
and depends upon, the residual sinks of deprived populations in the inner
areas of cities. Urban geographers now pay greater attention to the sociological aspects of towns, and they study social defectiveness, social segregation and the distribution of wealth, facilities, external economies
and diseconomies. Such studies cannot directly ameliorate the polarities
in urban society, but, like the observations of the nineteenth-century
commentators, they might reveal the obverse side of the urban coin. To
understand, and to make potential contributions to the achievement of
greater social justice, we need to turn away from a preoccupation with
static geographical patterns of urban society and look instead at the
processes and mechanisms which perpetuate social divisions within towns.

1 The residential kaleidoscope

It may be trite to say that social areas are composed of people living in houses distributed in space, but this definition embodies three vital components of residential areas and they are intermeshed together in a very complex way. The main focus of urban social geography is to try to unravel this complex weave. One way in which to approach the task is to look for simple geometrical patterns; to hunt for concentric circles or sectors or nuclei. This quest has a long history and from it have come many of our current ideas about the structure of social areas. There are two main strands involved; the economic and the sociological.

The economic approach

The economic approach stems from the work of land economists at the turn of the century. More recent writings (Alonso, 1964; Muth, 1969) have added some sophistication, but few radically new ideas, to these early concepts. Reduced to its simplest the argument involves two assumptions. First, it is argued that town centres offer maximum accessibility to the whole urban area and to all of the facilities and population of the town. A more central site will therefore offer a more attractive location for any type of land use than will a more peripheral site, so that competition for central land will be more intense and the prices offered will be higher. This competition will be heightened by the fact that, since the circumference of a circle increases by a multiple of the radius, there will be increasing numbers of sites at greater distances from the town centre and, conversely, fewer more central sites. The second argument is that each type of land use is able to put a financial cost to its evaluation of relative centrality and that these will differ from one type of land use to another. Firms and shops can quantify the extra custom which will come from a more central site; households can quantify their budgets and take into account the extra cost of travelling from more peripheral sites; and for each the utility of less central sites will decline at a different rate. Each land use will therefore have a characteristic *slope* to the amounts which it is prepared to bid for land at progressively greater distances from the centre. The hypothetical bid-rent curve will therefore fall rapidly away from the centre, and land uses will be sorted into an essentially concentric pattern with those with the steepest bid-rent curve being found in the most central sites. These central land-users will be retail and commercial activities which can best capitalize the necessarily high cost of central land. Residential land will be found in more peripheral locations, and the density of population and the intensity of land use will decline outwards as households buy larger amounts of less expensive land. Given two types of household, a richer and a poorer, it will be the poorer who lives in the more central areas since, given that travelling cost is a fixed item, it can achieve its lowest total outlay by reducing travel costs to a minimum and 'buying' only small amounts of land in central sites, thus living at high densities. The rich, on the other hand, will live at greater distances from the centre, will spend large amounts on travel, but will live at low density on cheaper land. Land and commuting costs are therefore seen as substitutable. This simple model can be varied or complicated in a number of ways: in addition to assuming a positive preference for more central sites, one can incorporate a positive preference for living at lower rather than higher density (Casetti, 1967); different types of transport, each with different speeds and costs, can be introduced, and the cost of time spent travelling can be added to the more basic travel cost (Lave, 1970); the restrictive assumption that work and amenities are only found in the centre can be relaxed by incorporating out-of-town and suburban shopping centres and work-places; different types of households, with differing ages, sizes, and incomes, can be introduced (Evans, 1973). In such ways the initially strict assumptions can progressively be relaxed to produce more complex versions of the basic model. All of these variations however, are merely twists to the basic micro-economic model which assumes that land users have typical bid-rent functions, and that there is an equilibrium solution to the competitive bidding between them, and that it is this which, instantaneously, produces the patterning of urban areas. The micro-economic approach to household location suffers equally from its assumption that housing markets operate through perfect competition and achieve an equilibrium position: but housing, in fact, is partitioned into distinct sub-markets, households express different sets of preferences, public policies interfere with economic processes, location is a unique attribute of any house (Kirwan and Martin, 1971). While the economic approach has thrown much light on the complexities of supply and demand, there is therefore scope for a more sociological approach.

The sociological approach

The second strand is the more empirical and descriptive one which stemmed initially from sociology, and which has tried to discover concentric circles, sectors, or whatever type of spatial pattern, and then tried to explain the pattern in inductive terms. The idea that urban land uses form patterns of concentric circles has a very long history. Engels's comment on Manchester in *The condition of the working classes in England* was written in 1842 and is often quoted. The central areas outside the commercial centre are, he said:

unmixed working people's quarters, stretching like a girdle, averaging a mile and a half in breadth, around the commercial district. Outside, beyond this girdle, lives the upper and middle bourgeoisie, the middle bourgeoisie in regularly laid out streets in the vicinity of working quarters . . . the upper bourgeoisie in remoter villas with gardens.

Charles Booth, later in the century, made similar observations about South London in his massive survey, *Life and labour of the people of London:* 'This huge population . . . is found to be poorer ring by ring as the centre is approached . . . While at its very heart . . . there exists a very impenetrable mass of poverty.' The most fully elaborated ideas about such patterns, however, came from the human ecologists of Chicago at the end of the First World War. The concentric circle model was spelled out in detail by Burgess and gave spatial expression to the 'natural' ecological processes which Park had written about so extensively (Park *et al.,* 1925). The dangers of drawing interpretations from spatial patterns can well be seen in the different conclusions which Engels and Burgess reached on the basis of this common geometry. Engels saw the 'hypocritical plan' as a concomitant of class structure and of the production and expropriation of economic surplus in a capitalist society. It provided a means by which the rich could live in pleasant surroundings at the outskirts and yet at the same time, since the main streets into the centre of the town were fronted with shops which were run by members of the lower bourgeoisie, could travel to the town centre without being exposed to the grime, the stink, and the poverty of the working population whose labour produced their wealth. Burgess interpreted the pattern (in the very different demographic context of Chicago) as being the product of the gradual assimilation of successive waves of immigrant populations who, as they were incorporated into the mainstream of American life, gradually moved from more central to more peripheral houses by a process of invasion and succession. As they moved outwards, so the social organization of their communities strengthened, family life increased, and, conversely, the social chaos characteristic of the central 'ports of entry' waned.

A superficially different geometry was suggested by Hoyt (1939), who worked from a background of urban economics rather than sociology. Hoyt added a directional element to the structure of land uses by stressing the sectoral pattern of towns, but this model of the town is not as radically dissimilar from the concentric model as has often been suggested; both depend upon the effects of centrifugal movements of households, and both recognize a similar gradient of status in which the higher-income families tend to live in more periperal locations. The mechanism of change in the two is different, however. Burgess emphasized the way in which lower-income households invaded residential areas and so displaced and succeeded the earlier communities; Hoyt stressed the process by which houses became less desirable over time and their residents moved to newer and better housing, leaving their original houses to 'filter' down to lower-income populations. In both models the sequence of events is the same, with houses filtering 'down' and people filtering 'up', but the catalysts of the change are different.

The attempts to suggest which of these two models is 'true' have been innumerable, but equally they have largely been misplaced, since the differences between the models stem very much from the differing focus of each: the human ecologists were interested in sociological questions, and, with their rather prurient distaste for large towns, they concentrated on the effect that urban life had on the strength of social control and on the family in its process of adjusting to city life; Hoyt concentrated more on housing and economic aspects, partly prompted no doubt by the fact that he worked to a brief given by the Federal Housing Authority, which wanted to know which houses were likely to be the safest investment prospects for their mortgage loans. As soon as we think of the structure of cities not in terms of the pattern of such single variables, but in terms of a whole variety of variables, any single city can at one and the same time show both a concentric and a sectoral pattern. It has been suggested that the patterns of variables related to income, with which social status is closely correlated, tend to form sectoral patterns, whereas variables related to the size and age structure of families tend to form concentric patterns (Anderson and Egeland, 1961). This dichotomy closely matches the different emphases of Hoyt and Burgess and so helps to reconcile their differences by seeing the city as a spider's web consisting of both sectors and circles.

Such simple geometries are obviously grotesque over-simplifications of the structure of towns and of the processes by which social areas are formed and change. To get some more faithful idea of the reality of social areas we need to look more closely at the processes rather than the spatial patterns, even though physical space, geometry, and spatial associations may be central to our interests as urban geographers.

At it simplest, geographical concern in looking at social areas resolves itself into three types of aspect and the three relationships between them; we try to understand the intermeshing of *housing space* and *social space* within the context of *physical space* (Fig. 1.1). What sorts of houses are lived in by what types of households and in what locations are they found? First we must look at the housing stock of a city. What sizes and types of houses does it have; what is the distribution of their prices; what sorts of physical amenities do they have; how are they distributed amongst the various types of tenure? Second, what is the social composition of the population of households? What are their size, their age, their occupational and income distributions; do they share accommodation or live separately; how much education have they had? These two sets of questions provide the first inter-relationship, between the social and housing characteristics. Do households with large numbers of children live in particular types of houses; do people with little formal education live in lower-priced houses? Third, we need to introduce physical space which gives us our other two inter-relationships. Are certain socially distinctive households found in particular locations? In practice, of course, most data are provided not for individual houses and households but for spatially defined groups (for example, the enumeration districts used in census data), so in most of the

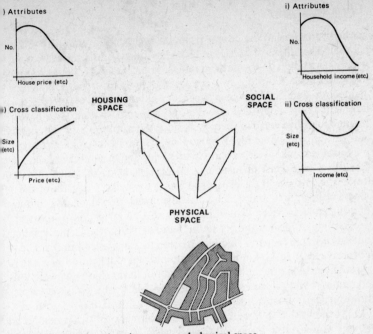

FIG. 1.1 Social space, housing space, and physical space.

studies of social areas the conceptually separate aspect of physical space tends to become conflated with social and housing space. It is nevertheless useful to think of the three as being separate, since this clarifies what it is that the social geographer is interested in.

Housing space

As houses age they lose value; newer styles come into fashion, bricks crumble, worm and beetle attack the wood, roof tiles need replacing, cement needs pointing. In general, the 'life' of a house is about 100 years, with little or no decline in its value over the first 20 years and thereafter a loss of some 1½ per cent each year. The social value of houses can, however, vary widely: Georgian styles may come back into fashion and so 'justify' the investment of capital to prolong their life; particular households may take less care of the fabric of a house or may reduce confidence in the expected future stability of a house or an area and so 'justify' less capital investment; society's or planners' ideas about acceptable housing standards may change; the ratio of total houses to total population may decline and so 'justify' the continuing use of houses which would otherwise be destroyed. Nevertheless, the great majority of houses in Britain are less than 100 years old (the percentages are: postwar 42; interwar 23; pre-First World War 35; some 19 per cent were built before 1891). This stock of houses has been built in a long series of booms and slumps in the building industry, and there have been some marked variations in the booms from one region and from one town to another. The stocks of houses in different towns can therefore vary very widely depending on the demographic and the economic history of any particular place. Consider two extremes. Bath has a large stock of eighteenth- and early nineteenth-century houses, many of which are large and easily subdivided into multiple accommodation. They have reached a critical stage in their lives, since their upkeep is very expensive and yet, since they are highly valued architecturally, there are strong pressures for their preservation. Sunderland, on the other hand, had until recently a large stock of small artisan cottages, many of which were built quite substantially in the prosperous years of the final quarter of the nineteenth century, but which have fallen below the standards of today' housing and have been demolished and replaced in a vigorous postwar programme of local authority house building. Variation in the age distribution of houses is paralleled by variation in the type of houses. The notorious back-to-back house, for example, was not found universally throughout industrial cities: London did not have many; nor were they common in every northern industrial town. Many of the textile towns, however, built most of their artisan houses to this pattern. Beresford (1971) shows that in Leeds, even in 1920, as many as 70 per cent of all houses were back-to-back, and that, despite the general ban on their construction after 1909, they were still being built in Leeds until 1937. Pre- and postwar clearance policies have now made such houses virtually non-existent. In other towns, different styles of house prevail: the 'tunnel back' is one such; in Tyneside a common type was the 'two-up, two-down in Wearside, the single-storey cottage. The variety depended upon local tradition and upon the guidance or the edict of housing acts.

The stock of housing in any town is also clearly affected by the social composition of the town (thus introducing the dimension of social space) The connection can be obvious, as in the sparseness of large, many-roomed houses, which can readily be converted into 'rooms' or multiple occupancy in towns which were overwhelmingly composed of manual households; or it may be more perverse, as in Cambridge where college fellows were forbidden to marry until 1871.

Such differences between the housing space of different towns can have effects over long periods because local authorities have been encouraged to pursue clearance policies more or less vigorously and at earlier or later dates depending upon the stock of houses within their boundaries. The number of local authority houses per thousand population can therefore vary widely: in Bournemouth the figure is 34, in Southend and Blackpool 36; on the other hand the figure for Sunderland is 141, for Sheffield it is 126, for Newcastle 125, for Wolverhampton 121, for Liverpool 114. And the timing of clearance programmes, which is partly prompted by the state and type of the earlier stock of housing, equally affects the age-distribution of these houses: in Birmingham, Nottingham, Bolton, Sheffield

Liverpool, Wolverhampton, Manchester, and Bradford, for example, the percentages of local authority houses which were built after 1945 vary between 50 and 60; whereas for Sunderland, Southend, Portsmouth, Luton, and Bournemouth the figure is over 80 per cent.

Since houses are so relatively permanent, and since the earlier stock of houses affects the date and type of houses which replace or add to them, this historical imprint of housing space, together with the new houses which are built in a town, stamps a most important template on the structure of a town and on the different areas within it. The characteristics of the stock of housing is a vital preliminary to any study of social areas since it provides the set of housing opportunities which facilitate or frustrate a household in its attempt to match its needs and aspirations with its housing space.

Social space

Whereas housing space affects the supply side of the housing market, social space, very crudely, provides the demand side. There are many aspects of a household's social composition which should be borne in mind; occupation, income, size, age, ethnic origin, migration history. It is in terms of such attributes that households select different types of houses in different locations within a town. Again, as with housing characteristics, there is a great deal of variation between towns in these social characteristics. Moser and Scott (1961), for example, conveniently show the ranges from highest to lowest amongst all of the larger towns in England and Wales in 1951. The percentage of people in the Registrar General's 'socio-economic groups' I and II (essentially the professional and managerial occupations) varied from a mere 7·7 in Dagenham to 45·4 in Coulsdon and Purley; the percentage of those in groups IV and V (essentially the manual occupations) varied from 10·1 in Southgate to 43·6 in Bootle; the percentages of people who left school before the age of 15 varied from 33·6 in Beckenham to as high as 86·2 in Stoke on Trent; one-person households varied from 3·7 per cent in Dagenham to 20·3 per cent in Hove; six-or-more-person households varied from 4·0 per cent in Southgate to 17·4 per cent in Huyton with Roby; the percentage of the population aged 0—14 ranged from 15·8 in Hove to 31·1 in Huyton with Roby; the population aged 65 and over ranged from 4·9 per cent in Dagenham to 24·6 per cent in Worthing. One could go on adding to such a catalogue of social statistics, but the interesting features are that the range of any one characteristic is so wide, and, as some of the above examples illustrate, that the same towns may often be found at the extreme ends of these ranges, suggesting the obvious fact that many of such social characteristics are highly intercorrelated.

We should also be interested in the changes of certain of these variables over time. Is the population of a town growing rapidly; how is its occupational composition altering; is the distribution of incomes growing greater or less, and how does the average income change in relation to changes in the cost of living? Such changes obviously affect the needs o the population of households and, also, its ability to buy housing of a particular sort. It is therefore natural that such demographic and social projections should play a large part in any calculation of housing situat and in evaluations of the social areas of towns (Dennis, 1970). With ma of the social variables, however, the simple notion of demand and supp becomes rather complicated since one cannot think of the social and housing spaces as interacting in such a one-way fashion. The number of households which need accommodation cannot, for example, be thoug of as a given item in calculating a balance of houses and people. People have married at increasingly earlier ages, they have had fewer children, and have formed progressively smaller households over time. The fall in the size of the average household has been very dramatic and is the product not only of purely demographic changes such as declining fertility but also of such social changes as earlier marriage and the setting up by young single people and newly-weds of households separate from their parents. Such changes depend upon houses being available for such households; the households are dependent upon the houses, so that, to some extent, supply creates its own demand.

Here, again, it is important to recall that the relationship between housing space and social space is a two-way inter-relationship, and henc the double-headed arrows in Fig. 1.1. We have already noted that the social composition of a town can affect the range of house types that th town will have. Conversely the absence of a particular range of housing types might well frustrate the aspirations of certain potential or latent households. This is best seen when we incorporate physical space and look at the way in which, for example, immigrant households or studen households have been channelled into particular areas of towns by the availability of particular sorts of housing. The areas of large decaying Victorian or Edwardian houses frequently act as the initial reception are for immigrant populations and often subsequently guide the direction o future expansion of such population. Likewise, the locations of new universities have introduced to a number of towns a radically new population element, which often was ill catered for by the existing housing stock. It was inevitable in the case of Lancaster, for example, that the majority of its students in its early days should find lodgings not in Lancaster itself, but in Morecambe with its stock of large, often subdivide houses.

Physical space

To these interests in housing and social space, geographers add a conscious interest in physical space. Are the house types and the household types distributed spatially in a particular fashion and how do they match together in space? Here the amount of work in geography is very considerable and it has continued the interest of the earlier human ecologist beit in the rather different guise of what is somewhat infelicitously known as 'factorial ecology'. This has developed out of the writings of hevky and Bell (1955), who argued that the mosaic of social areas in owns could be 'collapsed' into three independent dimensions which ould be measured by seven variables. The criticisms levelled at this heory' helped to lead to the use of many more variables and to a technique to group them into 'dimensions' which was not guided by a preonceived theory about the nature of the social and economic structure f cities. The multi-variate methods of factor analysis and component nalysis seem ideally suited since the techniques start with a large number f variables and reduce these to a smaller number of 'factors' or 'dimensions' which are composed of linear combinations of the variables. Physial space underlies the use of this approach since the data which are used efer not to individual households but to areal aggregates of households enumeration districts, census tracts, wards, or some other grouping, sually as used for census reports). The fact that dimensions are found a any factorial study of a town is therefore a reflection of the tendency or certain economic and social variables to show patterns of spatial ssociation; in other words, that the housing space, the social space, and he physical space cohere and interact in some way.

There are now many factorial studies of cities from a wide range of eveloped countries as well as a few from less developed countries. The ultural differences between these countries certainly produce differences etween the dimensions which are found, but, despite this, it is possible o see a common pattern for the cities of developed countries. This universal' model of urban structure (Sweetser, 1969; Robson, 1973) uggests that the spatial sorting of residential areas can be described by wo independent dimensions; the first is socio-economic status (which is nost simply measured by occupation) and the second measures aspects f the life-cycle of families (in terms of such variables as age distribution nd fertility ratios). These two dimensions—or variations of them—appear o be important in cities throughout the developed world and, for British ities, they can be seen in studies of London, Liverpool, Sunderland, Cardiff, Swansea and Birmingham. In addition to these two basic dimensions, others do appear, but they tend to be much more peculiar to the articular society which is being studied and can be thought of as additional 'filters' which, as a result of the particular cultural background, roduce multiple housing markets of various sorts. Thus, in the United States, the segregation of black populations emerges as a strong additional dimension and it reflects the way in which black households are effectively debarred from competing for housing and locations for which they would ave competed, given their income and socio-economic status and their osition in the family life-cycle, had they been white. For Britain, a somevhat comparable filter exists in the distinction between public and private ousing tenures. Local authority houses provide better physical amenities

than do privately rented or owner-occupied houses at comparable leve
of rent or mortgage repayment. Households who qualify for local auth
tenancy tend, therefore, to live in better housing than do households v
comparable income and family size who live in privately owned housir

The general structure of residential areas in British cities can theref
be seen in terms of the cross-cutting of three major dimensions: socio-
economic status and life-cycle, which are the two 'universal' dimensio
found so widely in cities in other countries, and a third dimension, mo
specific to Britain and arising out of the extensive development of loca
authority housing, which measures differences in the amenities of the
housing (Fig. 1.3, see below p. 27). Since the first two dimensions app
to be so general, let us look briefly at each in turn in some greater deta

Socio-economic status

Social status is a complex concept, and the relatively simple gradin
of status groups by occupations very often bears little relationship to l
individuals themselves view the structure of society or their own place
within it. People appear to use two types of criteria: either a 'power-ba
view of society in which, compatible with the Marxist view of social cl
they recognize a dichotomy between workers and bossess—a distinctio
which is clear in the use of the terms 'we' and 'they'; or a 'prestige-bas
view in which more divisions are usually recognized, the individual pla
ing himself in the middle range of categories. In this latter view, or in
views which mix both the power and prestige components, elements o
income, life-style, education, and occupation are all intertwined. The f
that people of similar status tend to live together is obviously deeply e
bedded in the individual's self-placement within his view of society. Th
reasons for social segregation can thus be seen as a reflection and a rein
forcement of a family's self-estimation of its own social standing. Und
lying this, according to Beshers (1962), is the attempt to perpetuate
social-status distinctions by living near one's own 'kind' and thus reduc
ing the chances of children meeting and marrying people lower in the
hierarchy of social status. More generally than this, one can argue that
people with high income will seek to pre-empt locations with positive
externalities (greenery, quiet, lack of industry, good cultural amenities
good schools) and leave areas with negative externalities to poorer hou
holds (Cox, 1973).

Social segregation can, then, be seen primarily as a way in which sta
distinctions in society are made clear and reinforced. In situations whe
status differences are very pronounced, residential segregation may be
less necessary as a further means of pointing the distinctions, as in the
tendency for racial segregation to be less marked in southern than in
northern American cities. Perhaps one can see something of the same i
Britain in the tendency for social segregation to become more marked
over time as social distinctions have become blurred. The nineteenth

entury city includes many examples of small-scale mixing of different
roups, as in the mews which lay behind many of the houses of the
vealthy, or the slums which were set in the midst of affluent suburbs—for
xample, the juxtaposition of Noting Dale Potteries and the prosperous
uburb of Kensington, the former being a custom-built slum 'sustained by
kind of bilateral trade with its affluent neighbours' (Dyos and Reeder,
973). Again, of course, the social and housing spaces interact to rein-
orce each other. If there is a belief that people prefer to live close to
imilar people, house builders will tend to build similarly priced housing
1 given areas, thus reinforcing the social segregation.

Certainly the evidence of such segregation is very clear, over and above
he suggestion of the factorial ecology studies. The larger the town, the
igher tends to be the degree of social segregation, but it is evident in
ven relatively small towns. Interestingly, it appears to be status rather
han simply income which determines such segregation. This is most
lainly seen in studies which look at the location of the better-paid man-
al and the lower-paid white-collar groups. Despite their lower incomes
he white-collar families tend to live in 'better' areas—a tendency which
)uncan and Duncan (1955) noted long ago in Chicago and which is re-
eated in Britain. The force of social segregation can also be seen rather
learly in situations where official policy has been to try to suppress it.
Ieraud (1968), for example, looks at the situation in a British New Town
n which the avowed intention was to produce a 'social balance'. By comparison with social segregation in other towns, the extent of social segre-
zation in Crawley New Town is considerably less. We can see this, and
nake a crude comparison between British and American towns, by look-
ng at the index of segregation, which has a higher value the greater is the
egregation (the comparison being very crude partly because the measure
lepends upon the size of the areas used in the calculation). For Chicago
here is a clear U-shaped pattern with the 'top' and 'bottom' ends of the
ocial hierarchy being most segregated: the figures for eight status groups
tarting with the 'highest', are 30, 29, 29, 13, 19, 22, 24, 35. For Oxford,
ising the five socio-economic groups of the Registrar General, the figures
re 35, 25, 13, 8, 18, which suggests more of a J-shaped distribution, with
he lower segregation of the 'bottom' end of the hierarchy being largely
he result of the building of local authority housing (Collison and Mogey,
1959). For Crawley, the pattern is much less clear, with figures of 17, 17,
5, 22, 13. However, despite this apparent success in reducing the level of
segregation, Heraud suggests that people have voted with their feet and
have begun to re-create a more segregated situation: the building of private
housing has created 'middle class' areas within the town; and also the
movement to peripheral villages has shown marked over-representation
of 'middle class' migrants.

The tendency for segregation by social status thus seems a well-
established pattern in the creation of residential areas. This continuing

tendency lends some additional support to the idea that, despite the growing affluence of many members of the 'traditional' working class, the difference between white-collar and black-collar occupations is still very real one in modern Britain. The thesis of *embourgeoisement* had suggested that, as they have earned more money, so many manual wor have adopted 'middle class' values and become indistinguishable from manual workers. Goldthorpe and Lockwood (1969), however, suggest this is altogether too simple a view. They argue that if this process is ope ating, it is most likely to be found in areas where 'traditional' occupati such as coal mining do not dominate, and where long-established and residentially immobile workers are not found. Consequently they studi workers in Luton and distinguish between three aspects of status; econ normative, and relational—relating to wealth, beliefs and life-style, and patterns of social contact. Despite the undoubted changes in the econ omic aspect they suggest that differences are still marked in the other two aspects. If there has been a blurring of social distinctions, it has be the result not of affluent manual workers assuming non-manual patter but of a convergence produced both by the changes amongst the bette paid manual workers, and by changes in the lower-paid non-manual workers such as their greater readiness to adopt unionist approaches in work situations. Britain is still a country with relatively low social mobility (Beshers and Laumann, 1967), and it continues to show mark segregation by social status.

Life-cycle

There is certainly considerable evidence, independent of the factori studies, that there are distinctive patterns of age distribution in cities. Jones (1960) shows the markedly different age pyramids in different areas of Belfast. Westergaard (1964) shows that, in the outer suburbs o London, there are 'ideal types' of suburban age structure. The logic of such segregation is that at different stages of its life-cycle a household has very different needs in terms of space and other facilities. A house-hold with young children will need space within the house, play-space close to the house, child clinics and schools within easy reach; a house-hold consisting of single people or of a retired childless couple may require less space, but may demand, in the first case, easy access to ent tainment, and, in the second, a large garden. The life-styles and the pre erences of individual households obviously vary widely, but, in general, one can see that there are needs which may well differ considerably depending upon the demographic structure of the household.

The difficulty in trying to study the pattern of such life-cycle differ ences is twofold. First, while it is possible to suggest ideal types of step in the life-cycle of *families,* it is difficult to aggregate this to a spatial pattern and argue about ideal types of *areal* life-cycle. An individual person ages progressively; a household changes both progressively as each individual ages) and intermittently (as new children are born and as individuals leave the household); an area can equally change both progressively and intermittently, with reversals in the ageing process being caused by younger families moving into an area which had been composed predominantly of older people. The concept becomes progressively more complicated as we change scale from the individual, to the group of individuals in the household, to the group of households in the area. However, we can suggest ideal stages in the family life-cycle, as in Fig. 1.2 where seven steps are suggested, running from the single-person 'family' or the childless newly married couple, through the birth of children; to the final stages of the older household whose children have left home to set up their own households. These stages are obviously idealized, but they suggest some common groups each of which suggests different housing and environmental wants. Next we can translate these ideal households into age structures. An age-segregated residential area

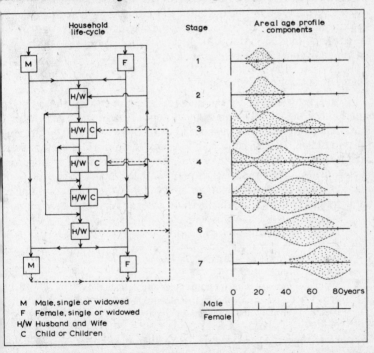

FIG. 1.2   Family life-cycles and the age profiles of urban areas. The left-hand side represents alternative routes through seven idealized stages. Dotted lines suggest the possibility that individuals or households reverse their progression by moving to join households formed by their offspring. The right-hand side suggests schematic age profiles which correspond with each life-cycle stage. The actual age profile for any given urban area may reflect one or some combination of these basic curves. *Source*: Robson, 1973.

might then be thought of as some combination of these age profiles. The second difficulty is to try to measure the age structure of a region, since as the age profiles suggest, the curves are very complicated, and the measures of age structure (such as people aged 0—14, or aged over 65, or the ratio of children under 5 to women in the child-bearing ages 15—45) reflect these curves only very crudely. The distribution of ages is not linear and it is therefore difficult to derive a single, unambiguous statistic to measure the age distribution of an area.

Despite these difficulties, the fact that residential areas do show markedly different age structures is apparent. In America, the tendency has even been commercially exploited by building age-group ghettos: Sun Cities, such as that in Arizona with a population of 14 000 and with no residents being allowed under the age of 50; apartment complexes called South Bay Clubs, with 60 per cent men and 40 per cent women, in which residents have to leave once they marry—and will doubtless then move to a suburban complex in which all of their neighbours will be at an identical stage in the life-cycle. British corporations may have been slower to exploit the situation than have American, but the fact of age segregation in British cities is nevertheless indisputable.

Aggregate structure of social areas

At an aggregate level, we can therefore think of British cities as being structured along these two main dimensions of status and of age, with a third dimension related to the housing differences produced by the multiple housing market of tenurial differences. If we think of each of these axes as being divided into two or three simple divisions, the cross-cutting of each division will produce a series of idealized 'boxes' such as in Fig. 1.3. Some of the combinations are less likely than others, and nine are suggested here each of which can be given a thumb-nail description:

Type 1	Interwar owner-occupied
Type 2	High-status owner-occupied
Type 3	Postwar semi-detached owner-occupied
Type 4	Postwar detached owner-occupied
Type 5	Student bedsitters
Type 6	Interwar council estates/inner-city council flats
Type 7	Postwar council estates/inner-city high-rise
Type 8	Privately rented low status
Type 9	Rooming houses

We can also suggest a very idealized spatial pattern of these residential areas, so as to describe the structure of a medium-sized British city (Fig. 1.3). The pattern combines both a sectoral and concentric form, with status differences being predominantly sectoral and age differences largely concentric, but with house tenure distorting this simple pattern. Three points might be emphasized in this geometric diagram. First, the high-status sector is shown running south from the centre. The highest

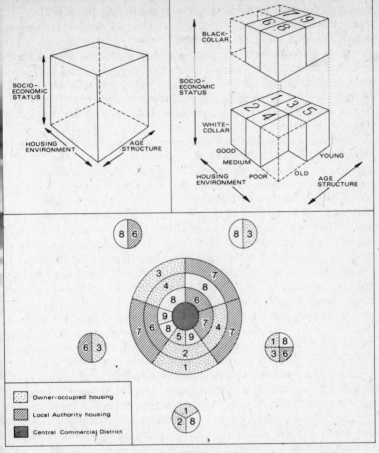

FIG. 1.3   Social, housing, and physical spaces in an idealized British city. Brief
descriptions of each numbered 'box' are given in the text. Even-
numbered 'boxes' contain predominantly older households; odd-
numbered 'boxes' contain predominantly younger households.

status area (Type 2) is of large Edwardian or interwar houses, is lived in
by predominantly elderly households, and is found in the middle rather
than the outer ring since such areas tend to persist over time and show
little outward movement. At its apex, this sector has been converted
into rooming houses with a polyglot population including low-paid
young households in cramped and subdivided houses, immigrant households, as well as students and young professionals living in flats and
bedsitters. Second, the inner areas have a very mixed population: rem-
nants of the 'traditional' working population living in rented housing

which has not yet been cleared in the continuing wave of urban renewal; immigrant households; a mixture of poor and of rich, but with few middle-income households; and numbers of council tenants, both older and middle-aged, living in a mixture of low- and high-rise accommodation. Third, the council tenants are distributed both in peripheral estates and in central redevelopment areas. The most striking differences between estates will be the age distributions, which will closely reflect the date of their construction so that, in general, the interwar and early postwar estates, often in the intermediate rings, will have households in the later stages of their life-cycle.

Beyond the administrative boundary of the town itself the peripheral villages must also be seen as containing a significant part of the 'town's' population. Most of the villages will be split between an indigenous population, most of whom will live in local authority housing, and an 'immigrant' population of commuters, who live in owner-occupied housing either in the form of older but modernized houses or of newly-built estates. What particular characteristics a village assumes will depend strongly on the attractiveness of the original village, its location (with a tendency, suggested in the diagram, for villages lying in the direction of the high-status sector to become the more affluent commuting villages), and the planning policies of the local authorities who will have designated some villages for growth and thus allowed the building of estates of private housing, and will have forbidden development in others so that they will either continue to be lived in by the indigenous population in rented accommodation or council housing, or will attract white-collar invasion through the conversion of existing 'desirable' properties.

This scheme is obviously played out with endless permutations in different towns, and the pattern suggested here is just one of a large number of variations. It does, however, suggest certain of the tendencies apparent in many British towns whose residential patterning is a complex product of the 'natural' process of residential segregation with a very strong overlay of control through planners, most strikingly apparent in the development and location of council housing. In looking at the spatial pattern of any town, one needs to bear in mind the interplay of the housing and social spaces. The actual spatial patterns which emerge in any one town will be strongly conditioned by the legacy of its past development, since housing provides a forceful imprint on the opportunities which are open to households. The legacy of history is strongly stamped on the spatial form of residential structure.

2 Housing demand: residential mobility

Having suggested some crude outlines of the aggregate pattern of residential areas in terms of the studies of factorial ecology, we have gone only a small way towards understanding social areas. We have described the end-product of a complex process by which households and housing interact in space. We need now to look in more detail at this process to see how social areas develop and change.

The total process is suggested in Fig. 2.1, which embodies the whole argument of this book and therefore warrants close scrutiny.

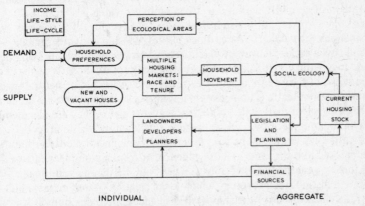

FIG. 2.1 Individual household mobility and the aggregate ecology of towns: the structure of the British housing market.

The three aspects of housing, social, and physical space are encapsulated in the boxes labelled 'new and vacant houses', 'household preferences', and 'social ecology', and it is their interaction in which we are interested. The first and most important dichotomy in the diagram is that between what may roughly be thought of as supply and demand: the availability of houses, on the one hand, which is subject to many constraints and influences through the role of planning and legislation, the availability of finance, and the activities of individual planners, landowners, developers; and, on the other hand, the housing wants of households, which, as we have seen in the last chapter, can be considered in terms of status (income, life-style) and age (the family life-cycle). Within this matching process there is a further constraint through the operation of multiple housing markets in terms both of ethnic differences and of differences in housing tenure.

The diagram also suggests a second dichotomy, between the two scale of individual and aggregate: on the one hand, the individual actors in the process (households, developers, planners, and so forth); on the other ha the aggregate effects both of the over-all ecology of the town, influence as it is by the existing stock of housing, and of the general impact of legislation. The relationship between these two scales is not one-way. Rather, as the diagram suggests, the arrows run both ways. On the demand side, the aggregate ecology is produced by innumerable individual household locational decisions, but it in turn influences those individual decisions through households' perceptions of the existing residential areas. Likewise, on the supply side, the provision of individual new and vacant houses is affected by general legislative fiats, but these in turn are formulated after consideration of the problems and the situation of the aggregate ecology of towns. In this chapter, we shall look at this two-wa relationship on the demand side by looking at the process of individual household mobility within the city; a mobility which produces the ecology of town, but is also influenced by that ecology. I am always struck by the parallel between this inter-relationship and, at a smaller and trivial scale, the way in which lecture classes develop their own micr ecology with a complicated, cross-cutting pattern of students segregated in terms of friendship, like interests, sex, and so forth. The neutral space of a lecture theatre is immediately given a social patterning once studen begin to select their seats. As further students arrive, they are faced with a limited number of vacant seats each of which now has some social significance—they may be next to a friend, someone of a different sex, a person from the same hall of residence, or from a group identified as sporting or academic or whatever. When full, the theatre will usually have a distinct social ecology which is the product of innumerable individual decisions but which has itself influenced those decisions as it evolves. This same, but continuing, process is suggested for towns by the diagram; the arrows run from individual households to the aggregate ecology, and a feedback runs from the social ecology to individual househe

Residential mobility

Do individual households consider social status and their family life-cycles as being most important in prompting their decision to move house and in selecting a new house to which to move? If it appears that they do, then the aggregate findings of the factorial studies can be seen as consistent with the aggregation of the decisions of innumerable individual households.

The amount of movement by households in Britain is very considerab Each year approximately 10 per cent of households move house. Since some households are highly mobile and others highly static, this does no mean that half of all households will have moved after a period of five years and all households will have moved after ten; rather, the figure works out to about one-third of all households having moved every five years (Table 2.1). Mobility in the United States is even higher than this, since approximately 20 per cent of households move every year in America. Any attempt to discover why these families move is faced with great difficulties of research methodology. Britain (unlike Sweden) does not have a register of household addresses from which one could plot household movements and find where households move to and at what stage. Researchers have therefore adopted one of two types of sampling framework to ask families why they move. Either they have sampled a total population, and have then been faced both with the difficulty that many of the families have not moved for very considerable periods and cannot validly recall the reasons for any moves that they might have made, and with the problem that families who say that they are likely to move in the future may not in fact do so; or they have tried to sample only people who have moved recently, by using town directories, electoral registers, or lists of other sorts. While much greater reliance can then be placed on the reasons given for the moves, this type of sampling design ignores the fact that many families who are identical to the recent movers have not moved house. The responses of these surveys must therefore address the question of why those who move do so rather than the more general question of why families either do or do not move.

TABLE 2.1 *Household mobility, Great Britain 1970*

Period during which head of household has lived in present house	%	No. of moves made by head of household in last five years	%
<1 year	10	0	65
1–4	25	1	21
5–9	18	2	7
10–14	14	3	3
15–19	9	4	1
20+	24	5+	1
		Not known	2
	100		100

Source: General Household Survey, 1972 (Total sample 796 households).

The most thorough surveys of recent movers' attitudes and reasons have been conducted in America, and Rossi's (1955) survey is the best known. He concluded that changes in family size connected with the life-cycle were the most important element in prompting household moves. Residential mobility, as he saw it, was a process by which families adjusted their housing to meet changes in their family size. Similar conclusions can be drawn for Britain. Table 2.2 shows the results of a survey of potential home owners who were asked by a building society the reasons for their move. The sample is therefore a very biased one, but the results are nevertheless of great interest. By roughly grouping the set of reasons

TABLE 2.2 *Principal reason for moving house*

		%
A. *Life-cycle reasons*		
	Getting married	33·1
	Increase in family size	1·9
	Decrease in family size	0·8
	To be nearer schools	0·5
	To be nearer social facilities	0·1
	Sub-total	36·4
B. *Career/income reasons*		
	Change in income	1·9
	Change in job	12·0
	Retirement	0·6
	To be nearer work	5·3
	More modern house	8·5
	Obtain garage	0·6
	Obtain better garden	0·7
	Seek better neighbourhood	3·9
	Sub-total	33·5
C. *Mixed and other reasons*		
	Accommodation too small	16·1
	Accommodation too large	1·6
	To be nearer shops	0·1
	To be nearer relatives	1·2
	Other	11·1
	Sub-total	30·1

Source: Nationwide Building Society, 1970 (Total sample approx. 5000 househol

we can allocate the great majority to one of two types: either reasons connected with the family life-cycle, or those based on changes in the career of the head of the household. Other reasons, such as the home being either too large or too small, might well refer to either one or oth of these two main types. Most of the reasons given for longer-distance movement between towns tend to be associated with the career argume people who move between towns constitute what Musgrove (1963) has tellingly called a 'mobile elite', the growing body of people with good education who move, rootless, from town to town, from one suburb to another, in search of better jobs or of career advancement. Those who move shorter distances within towns are usually prompted by changes i their family situation; by the birth of extra children, by the desire to m into the catchment area of a given school when their children reach a pa ticular age. Some of the intra-urban movement, however, is also connec to the life-cycle through more directly financial considerations, since th peak of earnings tends to be at the middle or later stages of a household life. Mobility can therefore be seen in terms of career and life-cycle, wit the former being more important in longer moves and the latter in shor moves.

Our interest can concentrate more especially on these latter, intra-urban, movers. Conceptual frameworks of their decision to move have been put forward by Chapin (1968) and by Brown and Moore (1970), and these are summarized in Fig. 2.2 which, even though difficult to convert into an operational model, does introduce some useful points for discussion. The decisions involved can be seen in two distinct stages.

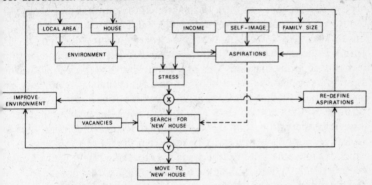

FIG. 2.2   The matching of family needs and housing: a conceptual model. *After* Brown and Moore, 1970

First is the decision to seek for a new house; second is the actual movement between houses. The catalyst which prompts the decision to seek a new house arises from stress caused by discordance between a household's needs and aspirations and the actual housing environment in which it lives. The environment will consist both of the house itself and also the local area (the physical environment of the immediate neighbourhood and the social environment produced by neighbours). The household's aspirations, as we have already seen, will be determined by its size, its income, and by its own self-evaluation of its social position. When stress reaches a critical point the family will decide to look for some better matching of environment and aspirations, and, at point 'X' on the diagram, will be faced with three alternatives. First, it can improve the environment: this could involve making alterations to the house itself, adding central heating, building an extra room, double glazing windows, persuading the landlord to repair the roof, taking in lodgers if the house is too large, applying for an improvement grant to install essential amenities; it could, on the other hand, involve communal attempts to improve the local area, by campaigning against traffic in the street, seeking better school or library or shopping facilities, campaigning for the local authority to designate the area as an 'action area', petitioning for the withdrawal of a licence from a non-residential land-user, forcing 'undesirable' neighbours or fellow-tenants to leave the area, or dissuading potential neighbours from becoming residents. The second alternative is for the household to lower its aspirations, and so come to terms with its current residential situation. This might involve, for example, a decision not to have a further child or to persuade part of the household (older childre elderly relatives) to leave the present household. Alternatively, it might involve a more general willingness to suppress aspirations in terms of the family's self-image, or, more commonly, to come to terms with the stre by 'putting up with' its present accommodation. Given the fact that surveys suggest that one-third of the population say that they would lik to move if they could and yet only 10 per cent do so in any one year, this latter situation would appear to be a very common one. The third option is the one which leads to the search for a new house and so to th second step in the diagram. This process involves matching the househo aspirations against the set of houses which are available. Again, very sin one can argue that, at point 'Y' in the diagram, three alternatives preser themselves: the first two lead again to improving the environment or lowering expectations, and they come about because the household's aspirations cannot satisfactorily be met from the set of vacancies at which it looks; the third option leads to actual movement into a house which provides a better matching than does the existing house.

This search process and the eventual decision either to move or to stay put introduces two topics worth discussing in some greater detail: first, the actual process of searching for vacancies, and second, the type of attributes of housing and of the environment which families take int consideration. On the first question, that of how families search for vacancies, there is considerable evidence that many people use very informal types of channels. Rossi (1955) suggested that, in his American data, the most used and the most successfully used sources were essenti informal. In Britain, the same is suggested by Herbert's (1973) survey in Swansea, which shows the relative unimportance of such formal channe as newspapers and estate agents, more particularly for respondents in a low-cost area. Sources which were successful in producing the house which was eventually moved to further reinforce this: for a high-cost ar the chosen vacancies were discovered by 'looking around' by 39 per cen of the respondents, 25 per cent were found through family and friends, whereas only 11 per cent were found through newspapers and 17 per ce through estate agents; and the difference was even more striking for a low-cost area, for which the respective percentages were 21 and 58 as against 13 and 8. The importance of the more casual channels suggests that it is more likely that households will search areas with which they are already familiar and, if this is so, that the 'action space' or the 'awar ness space' of households will play a not inconsiderable part in their selection of the area to which they eventually move. There are two aspe involved: first, the image that a resident has of particular areas of a city and, second, the areas with which he is familiar. On the first, Herbert's survey in Swansea again suggests some useful information. People's 'mental maps' of urban areas, like mental maps of the country as a who

Gould and White, 1974), appear to show certain similarities. The area immediately adjacent to their existing home is usually ranked high in their estimation; beyond this, certain areas of the city are generally agreed to be either desirable or not. On the second question, many studies suggest how partial and selective is people's use of urban space. An average commuter into a city centre might have a dumb-bell shaped awareness of his town, knowing in detail much of the area immediately around his home and some of the area around his workplace, with the two being connected by a narrow strip on either side of the routes which he habitually uses to travel between them. The underground traveller's mental map of London may be composed of entirely disconnected segments of space around each of the tube stations which he uses. Like a mole, he sees subterranean gloom except for those points at which he occasionally surfaces. This is the type of picture which Lynch (1960) has painted so compellingly of images of Boston and Los Angeles. Just as such images of cities differ, so do the areas with which individuals are familiar. Studies of people's movement and contacts in towns (Hägerstrand, 1969; Bullock et al., 1972) have constructed convoluted three-dimensional networks—like complex Hepworth sculptures—which show the difficulty of drawing general conclusions about individual movement in time and space. It does appear, however, that manual workers are familiar with a restricted area whereas white-collar workers have a much more extensive spread of contact (Chapin, 1965; Gould and White, 1974).

Such studies of individual use and awareness of urban space provide grounds for arguing that the search procedure of individual households may be spatially biased through the action space of individuals. Adams (1969) suggests that this leads to the elongation of the search space along an axis joining a household's present home and the central business district which would lead to a generally sectoral movement of households, and Brown and Holmes (1971) support this in suggesting that outer-city residents search for and choose new homes within a relatively small area around their existing homes, and that the area is generally elliptical and orientated around the same axis.

Housing chains

The houses that households would like to live in and the conceptual model of household mobility are, of course, very different from the types of houses that they do live in and the potential residential moves which are open to them. Households can only move house if they can find a suitable vacant property, but if they do move they may themselves create a vacancy by leaving their house empty for some future household to occupy. If we had a constant set of households and an unchanging set of houses, each move would generate a further move like some residential version of musical chairs. Since, however, certain households disappear and others emerge, and since houses are demolished and new houses built, the chains created by vacant houses will be truncated. We can think of a chain in the light of Fig. 2.3. It will have a starting and an e ing point and it will continue through time adding extra links to its len only so long as each move at time t_n creates a vacancy at time t_{n+1}. W can recognize a number of factors which either start or end such a cha As starting points, there are events which create a 'new' house and tho which cause the 'death' of a household. New houses can be created by new construction, by dividing existing houses into more household spaces, or by the conversion of property which had been non-residenti Households can dissolve through death, through the move of an existin household to share accommodation with some other household. Conve the end of a chain will be caused by the 'death' of a house or the birth a 'new' household. No further move will be created when a household moves from a house which is demolished, or from one which is conver to non-residential use, or which is incorporated into an existing househ space (by the conversion of a subdivided house into a single house, for example, or by knocking two houses into one), or if the house is left a a long-term vacancy. Equally, movement chains will end if the househo which moves into a vacant house is a new one and so leaves no vacant house. Most commonly this would arise through the setting up of a ne household through marriage where both partners had previously lived with their parents, but might also arise from the splitting of an existing household, or through divorced people setting up separate homes. The various causes are each listed in Fig. 2.3. Emigration and immigration, which are included in the diagram, are, of course, relative terms, and depend upon where the boundary of the study area is drawn. An immi grant into one area will end a chain in that area, but may start a chain the area from which he moved.

By the creation of such vacancy chains we can see that there is a po tential multiplier effect built into the movement of households (Donni 1961). The building of an entirely new house may therefore have effec which ripple through sets of further houses at lower links in the chain. is the set of initial vacancies created by chain starts plus these later link which, together, provide the set of vacant houses which enables resider mobility. What causes and what ends chains will, of course, depend par on the housing conditions of a given town. For both the United States and for Britain, new housing probably accounts for about half of the t chain starts. In Britain, unlike America, chain ends are commonly the result of the demolition of houses. In West Central Scotland, for exam chains which started in the owner-occupied sector were ended by dem lition in 3 per cent of cases, by new households in 45 per cent, and by immigration in 18 per cent; for chains begun by local authority houses 55 per cent were ended by demolition, 19 per cent by new households and none by immigration (Watson, 1973). In general, the most commo cause of chain starts seems to be the building of new houses, and for cl

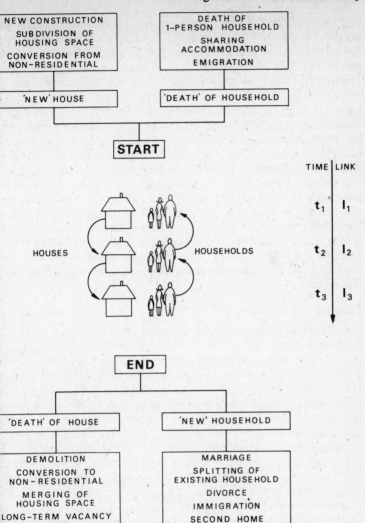

FIG. 2.3 Housing chains: the reasons why chains start and end.

ds the most common reasons seem to be the creation of new households
rough marriage and the demolition of houses.

There have been few formal studies of such vacancy chains, but
ansing *et al.* (1969) suggest, in a major study in the United States, that
e average length of chain started through new construction of private
using is 3·5. In Britain, Watson's study of chains created through new
ilding in both the private and public housing sectors in Central Clydeside

suggests a considerably lower average length: for owner-occupied hous
the figure is 2·0 and for local authority housing it is 1·6; the latter low
figure reflecting the high proportion of chains which are ended throug
the demolition of houses in the course of council building programmes
The length of these chains gives some indication of the 'benefits' to
households which are produced by building different sorts of housing.
Lansing's study, for example, longer chains were associated with highe
valued housing and with owner-occupied as against privately rented ho
ing: for owner-occupied houses valued at over $25 000 the chain lengt
was 4·5; for rented houses at less than $150 per month it was only 2·4
White (1971) likewise suggests for the United States that the building o
new subsidized housing will not have so large a multiplier effect and wi
not benefit the poor as much as will the building of middle-income private housing. In Britain, Watson suggests that building in the local auth
sector has shorter chain lengths, but affects households which are pred
inantly older, particularly 1- and 2-person households and those in the
lower socio-economic groups. A study of housing chains in Hull, howe
has found that local authority chains there are longer than private hou
chains (Gray, 1974).

Filtering

In such chains, we can see the way in which houses 'filter' down an
households 'filter' up the chain. The concept of filtering has a long hist
and refers to the progressive devaluation of a house through time. The
precise measurements of that loss of value can be made against a variet
of yardsticks: the change in the price or the rental of a particular hous
can be measured against changes in the prices and rentals of all houses
(Fisher and Winnick, 1951), against consumer prices (Lowry, 1960), o
against income (Grigsby, 1963). Ratcliffe (1949), who originally introduced the concept, linked his definition to a change in occupancy of a
house, and considered that it filtered down only when it changed hand
at a 'lower' value. In all of these definitions, each of which seems appr
priate in different situations, the same idea of houses moving up or do
in relative terms is the central point of interest. And we can see such p
terns in the data on vacancy chains. Lansing shows how successive fam
in any house generally tend to have lower incomes: 55 per cent of in-
movers have lower incomes than the out-movers; only 25 per cent have
higher incomes. Conversely we can see how families filter up, and this
again illustrates the points made earlier about the preference of househ
in their quest for housing. First, the standard of the housing improves
successive moves: 64 per cent of the houses moved to have more room
than the houses left, and only 17 per cent have fewer rooms; 52 per ce
of the households live at lower densities per room than they did in thei
previous homes, while 35 per cent live in more crowded conditions. Se
the life-cycle effects can be seen; in 41 per cent of cases, households m

TABLE 2.5

Family mobility and the career/life-cycle model in Britain

Life-cycle stage (see Fig. 1.2)	Age of household head	Family size	Median weekly income (£)	House size (bedrooms)	Tenure	Mobility (moves)	Possible location
2	24–5	2	35–40	2	Rent/own	1	Centre
3	26–30	4	40–45	2–3	Rent/own	2	Middle ring
4	31–40	4–5	40–50	3	Council/own	2	Middle ring/Periphery
4/5	41–50	5–3	50–60	3	Council/own	1	Periphery
5	51–64	3–2	45–50	3	Council/own	◁	Periphery
6	65–69	2	20–25	3	Council/own	◁	Periphery
7	(widow) 70–75	1	10–15				May move to live in home of married offspring

Notes: The table (inspired by a similar table for American data in Foote et al., 1960, p. 99) tries to show the career/life-cycle mobility for an 'average' family. It must be read with great circumspection. The 'average' man is a chimerical beast: demographic histories of individuals vary widely depending upon occupation and age at marrage, for example; income alters with age very differently in the cases of wage- and salary-earners; and house size and location vary with type of tenure. Indeed the whole argument of this book is that there is no 'average', since the housing market is so strongly partitioned. The life-cycle changes are based on current 'averages' which shows that bachelors marry at 25, spinsters at 23; that men survive to 69 and women to 75; that the 'average' woman has her final child by 27; that the average completed family size for a woman born in 1925 is 2·2; and that the average woman born in 1940 had given birth to 1·9 children by the age of 30.

Sources: Registrar-General Annual Report; Social Trends; General Household Survey; Census; Family Expenditure Survey.

into a house were at an 'earlier' stage in the life-cycle than the families moving out, while only 28 per cent were in a later stage. Obviously ther are many moves which run counter to our ideal model of residential mobility, but under the complexity of the patterns one can see the influence of the life-cycle and of improvements in household income.

Finally, one can also note the spatial effects of these moves, channelled through the successive vacant houses. Lansing looks at moves within a single city, Detroit, and shows how the average distance from the cent of the town decreases at each successive link in the chain: for the first link the distance is 18·2 miles, for the second 12·3, the third 10·7, the fourth 10·1, the fifth 9·9, and the sixth-and-greater it is 6·1. This reflect the fact that new houses tend to be built on the periphery of towns, but also suggests the way in which families move progressively outwards in the course of their residential moves.

The pattern of residential mobility is therefore a highly complex one but we can think of an ideal sequence which is suggested in Table 2.3, with families being prompted to move largely in terms of their position in the life-cycle, and gradually to improve their accommodation as their incomes rise to a plateau. Generally they move outwards, with some slight tendency for backward moves to be made in the later stages of the life cycle.

We can therefore see some of the constraints and some of the opportunities within the process by which households search for and move to new housing. In deciding to look for a new house, they are strongly prompted by a combination of job changes and, more particularly, of changes in family size (the so-called 'career/life-cycle mobility model') which ties in convincingly with the aggregate results of the factorial studies. And in selecting a new house, we can again suggest the importance of aspects related to income, to life-style, and to life-cycle, since the size of a house and the neighbouring environment of a house (the importance of the latter in residential preference being discussed, for example, by Kain and Quigley, 1970; Peterson, 1967; Whitbread and Bird, 1973) are both linked with income and with family size. To this extent one can argue that the individual preferences of households and the aggregate ecological structure of towns are closely in accord.

3 The supply side: multiple housing markets

The process of household mobility provides the link between the individual and aggregate aspects of urban residential structure. The process, however, is subject to a number of vital constraints which make the matching of individual needs and the types of housing in which households live far from perfect. The first of these constraints, which was suggested in Fig. 2.1 (see above p. 29), is produced by the multiple housing market in Britain, and is suggested in the factorial studies by the appearance of a dimension relating to the amenities of housing. In Britain there are two main types of multiple housing market: the first based on tenure, the second on colour.

Housing tenure

The importance of tenure is readily apparent in almost any index of housing or of social conditions. That one is dealing with virtually separate sub-markets can be seen in the flows of households between each of the tenure types. Fig. 3.1 shows gross flows of households both within and between four main tenure types (the residual category 'others' includes such relatively unimportant types as households who hold accommodation as part of their job). The two categories of owner-occupiers and council renters provide distinct end-points to the various moves between tenure types: flows move into them, but once a household lives in either type it rarely moves out, instead it makes moves within its own tenure. On the other hand, the two private rental categories act predominantly as feeders for owner-occupied and local authority housing. The pattern of moves is relatively simple. Newly-formed households move into owner-occupied housing or into one of the two rental types; the flow from furnished rented housing is predominantly to unfurnished tenancy, and from there flows are largely to owner-occupied or to local authority houses. There is a small 'leakage' from local authority to owner-occupied housing, but the ratio of moves within each of these two sectors in relation to moves from or to them is much higher than for either of the privately rented tenure groups.

These tenure categories play an important role in structuring social areas within towns and also in allocating resources within society. First, the amenities and standards of each type vary widely even when comparing accommodation which is 'bought' for similar outlays. There is great variety within each type, but it seems clear that better facilities are provided for comparable outlay by owner-occupied and local authority housing, and the worst by furnished rented housing. Second,

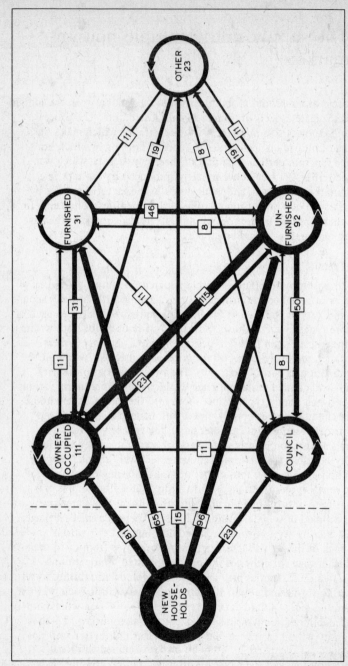

FIG. 3.1 Household mobility between different types of house tenure in England. For 1000 households, the numbers show the size of flows between each tenure; figures within each 'circle' show the numbers of households moving within that tenurial category. The width of each line is proportional to the size of flow. Data calculated from the Rowntree survey of

and connected with this, is the fact that the long-term financial implications of buying as against renting housing are highly favourable.
Third, the security of tenure differs: the most secure is owner-occupied
housing and the least secure is furnished rented accommodation, which
for long was unprotected by the various housing acts and was given a
degree of security only in 1974. Owner-occupied and local authority
houses are obviously the two most favoured types of tenancy, and this
is reflected by the varying satisfaction shown by different types of
household. The importance of such tenurial differences has been tellingly
embodied in Rex's (1967, 1968) concept of 'housing classes', which,
arranged in order of their desirability, he sees as follows:

1. Outright owners of large houses in desirable areas
2. Mortgage payers who 'own' whole houses in desirable areas
3. Council tenants in council-built houses
4. Council tenants in slum houses awaiting demolition
5. Tenants of private houseowners, usually in the inner ring
6. Houseowners who must take in lodgers to meet mortgage repayments
7. Lodgers in rooms.

One could think of a variety of other such 'classes' (Ambrose, 1974), and,
given the financial advantages associated with mortgage repayments, one
might question the respective positions of categories 1 and 2, but the
concept is a most useful one. The 'classes' can be seen as competing for
limited resources, the resources being the limited access either to mortgage capital for the owner-occupiers or to subsidized public housing in the
case of local authority tenants.

The changing balance of tenure types through time is a further indication of the present desirability of either owner-occupancy or of council
tenancy. Since the Census has only collected information on tenancy
since 1951, it is difficult to discover precise changes in tenancy before
this, but it is clear that there has been a most dramatic change from a
situation of almost complete private renting to the virtual disappearance
of private renting today. For example, in Leicester in 1914, 95 per cent
of the houses were rented privately and only 5 per cent were owner-
occupied; by 1971 private renting had fallen to a mere 15 per cent,
while owner-occupancy had risen to 50 per cent and council renting to
28 per cent (Pritchard, 1972). Likewise, in Ramsgate in 1851 a mere
20 per cent of houses were owner-occupied and the remaining 80 per
cent were privately rented (Holmes, 1973). Recent tenurial changes
(Table 3.1) show that this process still continues strongly and is producing a housing stock largely split between owner-occupied and council
houses. These changes in tenancy began before the First World War, first
with the start of state-subsidized council building on a large scale after
the Housing Act of 1919 and in particular after the Chamberlain and
Wheatley acts of 1923 and 1924, and, second, with the dramatic

TABLE 3.1 *Changes in tenure and regional differences in tenure, Great Britain 1966–72*

	Owner-occupied	Local authority	Privately rented	Other	Total
	% dwellings				
Great Britain, 1966	46·6	28·4	19·6	5·4	100
Great Britain, 1972	51·0	30·6	13·4	5·0	100
England, 1972	53·0	28·3	13·9	4·8	100
Wales, 1972	55·4	28·3	11·6	4·7	100
Scotland, 1972	31·0	52·9	9·6	6·5	100

Source: Housing and Construction Statistics, H.M.S.O., 1974.

expansion in private house building (almost all of which was for owner-occupiers) in the 1930s (Fig. 3.2). Subsequently, and more especially in recent years, the change in the balance of different tenure types has been continued further by the sale of many rented houses to owner-occupiers and by the demoliton of others.

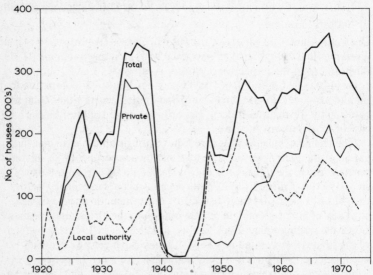

FIG. 3.2   Permanent houses built in England and Wales 1920–73. Data from Mitchell, 1962; *Annual Abstract of Statistics;* and *Housing and Construction Statistics.*

The reasons for the decline of tenanted housing are clear (Nevitt, 1966). The predominant causes are the financial advantages which public policy has given both to owner-occupiers and council tenants at the expense of the private landlord. The subsidy of council tenants is an obvious element. Since 1919, local authorities have been able to claim subsidies from the central government to supplement the contribution from their own local rates so as to provide housing which manual households could afford, without imposing too heavy a rate burden on the town itself. The amounts and form of these central subsidies have varied with successive acts (the first act, for example, gave a very open-ended Exchequer commitment to meet all losses in excess of a penny rate, and was soon abandoned in favour of a fixed subsidy for each new house built). There is therefore considerable variation from one town to another in the amount of subsidy which is paid, depending on the particular subsidy for which its housing qualified (and thus both on the data of its building effort, and on such factors as whether cheaper or more expensive central land was used) and what the prevailing interest rate was at the time of loan. The amount of the central subsidy in 1962–3 varied from as high as 12s. 1d. per pound in Chelsea to 3s. 2d. in Oxford; the local rate contribution varied from 10s. 11d. in the pound in Bethnal Green to a *credit* (in other words, money being put into the rate account) of 1s. 8d. in Eastbourne. The subsidies 'paid' to owner-occupiers are less obvious, but not necessarily less generous. They come mainly in the form of tax concessions on the interest paid on the building society loans or on capital and interest payments to insurance companies. Since the abolition of Schedule A tax, which was paid on the profits of selling a house, the absence of taxation on the rising value of property also represents a further and more hidden subsidy.

By constrast, the private landlord has progressively been squeezed out of the market through the operation of these financial policies. The fact that taxation policies and housing policies in Britain have largely been divorced from each other has been one of the main reasons for the decline of the private landlord, since subsidies in both the owned and the council sector have acted as twin prongs which have made the landlord's financial position untenable. The effect of the series of rent-control acts which first started in 1915 has, paradoxically, been to help preserve rather than eradicate the private landlord by making it difficult for him to sell his property. Conversely, acts such as the 1957 de-control of rent led to a greatly increased sale of rented houses as landlords chose to realize the capital which otherwise would have been tied up in their property. Interest rates and the rising price of housing have merely swelled this conversion of rented to owned houses. If interest rates stand at, say 10 per cent, a landlord can realize this rate by investing capital in the money market. The rents which he would have to charge to match this and allow for the costs of management, depreciation, and profit were he to keep his capital in housing, would be higher than comparisons with other tenure prices would allow. The comparison, of course, depends on the base which the landlord uses. Suppose he bought a house in the 1940s for £1000 and that he sought a return of 12½ per cent on that investment, if he charged that rate on the historic price of his property he would charge a rent of £2·50 per week, but, in a period of rapidly rising house prices, if he thought that his house would now sell with vacant possession for £10 000, and he used this as the basis of his calculation, he would need to charge a weekly rent of £25·00.

The flow of property from the rented and into the owned category has thus been controlled by the oscillations of public policy, with particular acts encouraging or discouraging the landlord from selling, but with a strong continuing financial logic impelling him to sell and retire from the rented market as soon as he is able. The consequences on the supply of cheap private property have been profound. Only in the case of privately rented furnished property has there been any tendency to increase the supply; for houses situated in the centre of towns it has been possible for private landlords to compete with building societies and local authoriti by charging very high rents which reflect the scarcity value of the site itself and thus represent a 'pure' rent for the land on which the house stands. Households willing and able to pay such rents have been small and usually white-collar—students, childless couples looking for central luxury flats. Taxation policy and the growth of building societies and local authority building have therefore had profound effects upon the traditionally large supply of cheap rented housing which once formed the bulk of central housing in towns and provided ready accommodation for new households and the manual population (Mellor, 1973; Glass, 1970). The continuing housing crises, particularly in the large cities, must be seen as reflections of the constraints and the controls imposed within the country's economy—a curious and ill-functioning combination of private capitalism and public subsidy.

Owner-occupation

The benefits of owner-occupation cannot be doubted, especially when house values have generally kept pace with or outstripped rises in general costs and prices. Again, however, it is instructive to consider the constraints which apply to this form of tenure, especially through the policies of building societies and other mortgage sources. Taxation policy helped to swell the assets of the building societies after the First World War (in the early 1920s investors only paid one-quarter of the standard tax rate on the interest which they received, and this encouraged both individuals and corporations to invest in the societies) and this, together with the low interest rates of the 1930s (from 1932 to 1939 the bank rate stood at a mere 2 per cent), opened the flood-gates for the expansion of private house building in the 1930s (Fig. 3.2). National policy and the policy of the societies are therefore critical in understanding the rise and the structure of the owner-occupier sector.

There are two interesting constraints involved in building society practice. First, the maximum value of a mortgage is usually only a percentage rather than the total cost of a house. Second, the size of a mortgage is usually determined as some relatively fixed multiple of an individual's income (usually up to three times his income, an amount which is determined by the fact that, in Britain, households spend approximately 15–25 per cent of their income on housing). The first condition means that individuals need to be able to raise capital in the first place to qualify for a mortgage, and this might discriminate against people with lower earnings who may be less able or less predisposed to accumulate savings. The second condition somewhat favours those who have a regular income and also have expectations that their income will rise progressively over time so that repayments will form a progressively smaller fraction. Again, the situation favours the white-collar worker against the manual, since the latter's earnings are more subject to fluctuations in terms of overtime and short-time working and his earnings do not necessarily have a built-in annual increment. Building societies might thus be predisposed to interpret the maximum that they will lend rather more generously in the case of the white-collar worker. Here, Barbolet's (1969) study of new private housing in Outer London is of interest since she suggests that, despite the fact that clerical workers (whom she calls 'marginal' middle-class workers) earn on average less than skilled manual workers, and buy houses which are slightly more expensive, they nevertheless get on average rather higher mortgages. The effects, if such policy is indeed widespread, will be both to deprive manual workers of access to capital and hence deprive them of the opportunity of benefiting financially from the rising price of property, and also to create a class of relatively poorly paid white-collar workers who, in the absence of a large stock of cheaper privately rented property, take out mortgages which they can barely afford for new houses in the suburbs and so become 'reluctant commuters'.

One of the most dramatic ways in which owner-occupied housing has replaced privately rented has been through the process rather unlovingly called 'gentrification' which has been widespread particularly in London, and has involved the buying-up and modernization of 'working class' houses by or for white-collar households (Hamnett, 1973). The wave of this 'invasion' has spread progressively outwards in the last ten years from central areas and from areas close to the historically fashionable inner areas such as Hampstead and Kensington, so that, particularly in once manual areas such as Islington and Greenwich, there has been a radical change in the social composition of local populations; house prices have risen considerably beyond the means of the manual workers; rented property has severely declined in quantity; and the early 'invaders' who have subsequently sold their houses have made a handsome profit. Rising house prices and the unattractiveness of rented property as an investment except for the 'luxury-flat' market have, of course, provided a strong 'logic' for such developments, and the activities of property companies in converting houses can be seen in this light, but a not inconsiderable part has also been played by public policy in the form of improvement grants. Standard improvement grants have long been paid to bring houses up to a defined level, so that assistance has been given for the installation of baths, running water, and other basic amenities. Discretionary grants, which are paid for general improvements to houses which meet these standards and which have a sufficiently long life, were made considerably easier and more generous after 1969, and they have doubtless helped to stoke the process of conversion of rented houses and of the invasion of areas by non-manual households. Since, until recently, there was no check on owners selling their improved houses, these grants could add both extra financial incentive to the activities of property companies and the promise of capital gain to private owners.

Local authority tenancy

The council sector provides the second of the two 'favoured' tenures. Before 1919 there was a small stock of local authority housing and of houses under the management of housing associations, but it was after the 1924 Wheatley subsidies that local authority housing began to assume significant proportions in the larger towns so as to create the present pattern of tenancy. Today, almost one-third of British houses are in local authority hands. Again it is interesting to look at the constraints which operate in this now considerable tenure sector.

Local authorities, as managers of the stock of council houses, have a certain amount of freedom both in terms of the number of houses which they build and of their subsequent management. We have seen already that there is considerable variation in the energy with which councils have pursued house building, whether for slum clearance or to meet general housing requirements. On the management side, the interesting question concerns the allocation policies of different authorities, where, again, there is great scope for local variation, since the Central Housing Advisory Committee, as its name suggests, only provides guidance in evaluating different selection policies, and Ministers of Housing have been reluctant to interfere in what is seen as a local matter. At one extreme, some authorities allocate housing on the basis of the length of time which a family has been on the waiting list; at the other, there are various 'point' scheme which try to provide objective bases for comparison (Cullingworth, 1966) Families displaced by slum clearance have priority in all towns, but the weighting of other criteria in points schemes—such as overcrowding, ill health, large family, length of residence in the area—can be very different The allocation of tenants to different types of housing—to flats as against terrace houses, to interwar as against new houses—is also in local hands, as are rental policies; for example, the costs of older and newer housing may or may not be pooled to charge an average rent which may or may not bear a relationship to the actual cost of the house itself. Since there is so wide a variation in local practice it is impossible to outline a 'standar council policy. There is, however, some fragmentary and rather impressio evidence that councils grade tenants and prospective tenants in social terms—in terms of cleanliness, the regularity of their rent payments—to divide them into 'good' or 'bad', irrespective of their housing need. Whether such gradings are then used to segregate bad tenants into older poorer housing and into particular 'problem' estates seems again to vary from authority to authority, though the practice seems not to be un-common (Kirkby, 1971; Tucker, 1966). There are obviously management advantages in doing this, since it means that families most likely to need the assistance of welfare services can more readily be contacted and since it is commonly argued that estates gravitate down to the lowest common denominator. Whether by such conscious policy or by less insidious pro-cesses, local authority estates—like housing areas in general—take on dis-tinctive images, some being seen as good estates and others as bad. These images, together with the changing housing needs of growing or contract-ing families, provide the rationale for the extensive transfers of existing local authority tenants from one council house to another.

These patterns, and the changes in the patterns of the different types of tenure, have profound effects upon the social areas of towns. The demise of cheap rented accommodation and the incentives or pressures for households to buy houses if they can qualify for mortgage advances have helped to polarize the housing market. Cheaper new housing is built in peripheral locations, so that, with the exception of local authority hous-ing, there has also been a spatial polarization, with the better-paid workers moving progressively to the suburbs and the poor being left in the centre. When this is allied to the fact that office jobs have diffused from town centres less rapidly than have manufacturing jobs, so that, of unskilled jobs in the centre, mainly the very lowest-paid service jobs remain, this spatial dichotomy takes on additionally serious proportions. The job markets and the housing markets are being pulled apart and the very poor are caught in a trap in the central city (Hall, 1973; Pahl, 1971).

Race

The second type of multiple housing market which must briefly be mentioned is based on colour. The significant and growing population of 'new' commonwealth immigrants in British cities cannot compare num-erically or in terms of their segregation with the black population of American cities, but there is certainly evidence of discrimination in its housing. The fact that the degree of segregation of immigrants is greater than would be expected on the basis of their socio-economic status alone is some indication of this (Lee, 1973). Whether such segregation is the product of antipathy on the part of the host society or of a preference on the part of the immigrant households must of its nature be difficult to establish, since the second might well be a reaction to the first. The great majority of immigrants have settled, not in the seaport towns of Cardiff and South Shields which had populations of earlier immigrants,

but in London and the industrial towns of the North West and Midland
where unskilled and semi-skilled work has offered incentive. Within the
towns they have settled predominantly in the 'twilight' areas adjacent t
the centre, where cheap accommodation exists and where large houses
have been subdivided and offer the possibility of dense but cheap accor
modation. Immigrants consequently live in areas of excessively poor
housing and particularly in areas of rented accommodation (Jones, 197
Dalton and Seaman, 1973; Haddon, 1970). There is here a cross-cutting
within the tenurial sub-markets at which we have just looked, since the
distribution of West Indian and Asian households amongst the various
tenurial categories is radically dissimilar from that of the total white
population. In areas of considerable immigrant settlement in both
London and Birmingham, for example, the coloured immigrants are
under-represented in the local authority and the unfurnished rented
sectors and over-represented in the owner-occupier and furnished rente
sectors. Figures for seven Inner London Boroughs in 1966 show 33 per
cent of the English population in council housing as against a mere 5 pe
cent for coloured, and 44 per cent English in unfurnished rented as
against 24 per cent coloured; conversely 22 per cent of coloured immigrants are owner-occupiers against 14 per cent of English, and 48 per ce
of immigrants are in furnished rented houses whereas only 6 per cent of
the English population are (Rose, 1969). Much of the rented housing is
owned by coloured landlords (Barnett, 1970) some of whom themselves
live in their own houses and sublet rooms (a category of housing class
explicitly recognized, and ranked very low, by Rex and Moore (1967) in
their study of the immigrant area of Sparkbrook). Such subletting is one
way of entering a tight housing market which might, in certain cases, be
made even tighter by discrimination or by the practice of charging highe
rents to immigrant households (Karn, 1969). By buying property immigrants ensure accommodation, but many have to buy through borrowin,
money from financial institutions other than building societies and are
faced with higher interest charges which can only be met by subletting c
by becoming property landlords. One of their principal mortgage source
in London and other of the larger cities, however, has been the local
authority whose terms are notably more relaxed than building societies.
The marked absence of coloured households in local authority housing
might partly be seen as the obverse side of this lending policy and of the
expressed preference of coloured populations for owning rather than for
renting property, as Davies (1972), for example, suggests in Newcastle.
But local authorities have certainly treated the prospect of allocating
coloured populations to council housing with considerable caution and,
even in drawing up plans for the clearance of inner areas, have tended to
avoid areas of denser coloured settlement (Burney, 1967; Deakin and
Cohen, 1970). Duncan (1974), for example, notes that, in defining
general improvement areas, councils are officially urged to give priority

the 'improvement of areas which will obviously repay attention', and that, in practice, this has been interpreted in the case of Huddersfield as meaning the avoidance of areas with large proportions of sub-standard housing and of coloured populations.

The danger of the working of the housing market, which has so strongly controlled the areas of coloured settlement, is that it exacerbates the tendency for the spatial concentration of immigrants and dampens the likelihood of their diffusing to less central areas as rapidly as the white households. This difficulty is heightened in the educational sphere, since, given the young age structure of coloured populations, schools in immigrant areas tend to have proportions of coloured children which are much higher than the proportion of coloured households in the area. Public policy on the question of segregation and de-segregation has favoured a cautious approach to conscious de-segregation. On the one hand, there are genuine reasons why concentration rather than complete dispersal might not necessarily be deplored. Local services can better meet any specialized needs of an immigrant population if it is concentrated: food shops and social services can be deployed more efficiently and the shared experience of living together in a society whose *mores* and life-styles may not be familiar may help immigrant populations to adapt to the host society. On the other hand, even though the concentrations of coloured households in British cities are at present far below the proportions of American ghettos, the spectre of more complete segregation and of racial tension is very real. As writers such as Cullingworth argue (Ministry of Housing and Local Government, 1969), the danger is that, even though there may be no causal connection between immigrant settlement in an area and the area's urban decay and the development of social *malaise*, the fact that immigrants are found so predominantly in such areas helps to establish a popular belief in the reality of such associations which helps to feed any latent mistrust, dislike, or xenophobia.

The current tendency for segregation of coloured households is, of course, paralleled earlier in time by the segregation of other immigrant groups, more especially the Irish (Jackson, 1963; Richardson, 1968). Today, the extent of such segregation of earlier immigrant populations is considerably less as they have become more completely integrated with the host society. So far as the Irish are concerned, however, the continuing role of religious, as opposed to national, segregation, so tragically manifest in Belfast, introduces yet a further form of multiple housing market (Poole and Boal, 1973). Differential access to housing, amongst other facilities, is one of the most evident grievances paraded by the Catholic population as an overt sign of a much deeper conflict. The cultural divides of streets such as the Falls Road are a striking spatial expression of social conflict which has been explored by Boal (1969).

Urban society has been changed considerably by the workings of the welfare socialism of postwar Britain, and any comparisons of present-day, prewar, and nineteenth-century cities must recognize the very great absolute difference in the life-styles and life standards of urban populations. The widespread abject poverty exposed by Booth and other nineteenth-century commentators has disappeared from today's cities. However, the relative range of differences in wealth and in social and physical environments has shown little evidence of growing narrower. Our yardstick should be a relative not an absolute one. As the general material welfare of society has increase, so, understandably and reasonably, have expectations been raised. Relative deprivation must be adde to our calculus as well as absolute deprivation (Runciman, 1966; Abel-Smith and Townsend, 1965). It is in this context that the constra imposed by the housing market need to be stressed and need either to eradicated or made less palpably unjust. The curious mixture of private capitalism and public welfare, through which the housing market opera creates inconsistencies and widens divisions in the allocation of what is social need, not a consumer luxury.

The supply side: managers within the system

Having emphasized the constraints in the supply and allocation of houses, it is already obvious that certain institutions and certain individuals play crucial roles in controlling the system. Even though population growth and new household formation are important on the demand side, for example, it is evident that the role of building societies and the general availability of mortgage capital and credit very largely dictate how great will be the pressure for houses at least in the private market. General governmental legislation, taxation policy, and the general state of the economy are equally important considerations in the complex intersection of supply and demand. In this chapter, we shall look briefly at the role of three specific actors—landowners, developers, and planners—who are included in the earlier diagram of the housing system (Fig. 2.1, see above p. 29) and who can be thought of as managers within this system. The power vested in their hands plays a considerable part in determining what sorts of houses are available and in what areas they will be found.

The development of residential areas is a sequential process in which rural land is converted to urban. Drewett (1973a) suggests seven steps in this process: from non-urban land use, through urban shadow effects, active interest, planning permission, land purchase, active development and, finally, to the purchase of houses. At each stage a different set of actors is involved; landowners, speculators, developers, planners, and consumers. At each stage, planning policy and the cost of finance (for buying land, for developing land, for the final house purchase) are vital general factors, but we shall look at the more specific roles played by landowners, developers and planners.

Landowners

Since the 'nationalization' of the use-rights of land (the right to do what one will with land that one owns), the scope for landowners to influence the course of residential development has obviously declined. There are, nevertheless, two principal ways in which landowners and the pattern of land ownership can play a part. First, the size of holdings can be of importance in determining the nature of development. For large-scale developments, it is obviously cheaper and easier to deal with land held by few owners than by many, and in large lots rather than small; not only are the legal costs less, but so too are the costs of the time taken to assemble land—the heavy interest charges and the opportunity costs of having capital tied up in part of an area awaiting develop-

ment. In nineteenth-century cities there are many instances of such
landholding patterns helping to guide the location of large-scale develo
ments; wherever possible, both the routes of railway lines into cities
and the location of the more comprehensively planned estates were in
areas in which land was held in few hands (Kellett, 1969). Where own
ship was fragmentary, development tended to be piecemeal and hap-
hazard and, more likely than not, to be of lower rather than of higher
residential status. In more recent periods similar tendencies can be see
Fragmentary land ownership on the fringe of urban areas has frequent
produced difficulties in the land's subsequent development (Grayler,
1970). But the chief instance of the influence of the size of landholdin
has been associated with the growth of larger-scale development, both
with the building of extensive local authority estates and with the rise
of large private building companies. Mortimore (1969) shows for
Bradford, and Ward (1962) for Leeds the way in which the location o
interwar council estates was guided by the location of land held in larg
units by a single owner.

Second, there is still scope for the landowner to impose his wishes
the type of development and on whether or not development takes
place. Again, this power was greater in the past (Carter, 1970). Restric
tive covenants are a common feature of many nineteenth-century
residential developments, and the different attitudes of landowners ca
be seen, for example, in the development, on the one hand, of middle-
income suburbs in North London guided by the insistence on high
standards of construction and layout by the landowner, Eton College,
and, on the other, the development of slums in Sheffield built on land
whose owner, the Duke of Norfolk, allowed building to take place wit
out any fetters (Olsen, 1973). Such different types of development are
often, of course, the product of the market potential of a piece of lan
since the simple act of adding a covenant to a land sale cannot ensure
that it will attract high-income households. Today, such restrictive
covenants are still sometimes imposed, but the landowner's role is a
much reduced one. They can be important in areas of leasehold land—
and extensive areas of London are still held in lease from large estates
such as the Grosvenor—but the role of the landlord is most critical in
determining whether or not land will be sold and at what price. The
landowner is usually under no compulsion to sell unless he needs to
raise capital or in the case of compulsory purchase. His decision to sell
will be influenced by how attractive other investment opportunities ar
and the price which he will expect will reflect the type of developmen
which planners will allow as well as his own estimate of future
expectations of house prices. Since, in a period of land shortage, developers desperately need land if they are to survive whereas landowners
are under no obligation to sell, the unequal position of buyer and selle
has the effect of forcing land prices up (Drewett, 1973b).

Developers

The developer today plays a much more active role as intervener. Given his need for land, it is he who has winkled land from its owners, and, given the high cost of holding undeveloped land other than for speculative purposes, it has been in his interest to build quickly, so that, in the private sphere, he has been the catalyst who has injected new houses into the system with all of the consequent multiplier effects on residential movement that we have already seen. The developer acts as interpreter of what the 'market' demands, and, although what is built is subject to the approval of planners, the developer's 'reading' of the market is therefore crucial. As large-scale companies have developed in the postwar period, so have scale-economies become possible in building large-scale standardized estates, and it is such housing that the customer increasingly has been offered. The planners do, of course, provide constraints on what the developer can build. Gracey (1973) suggests that the planner has seen his role as that of educating the developer in his own concept of 'correct' planning and layout, and, in the years since the 1947 Planning Act, the developer has increasingly worked in harness with the planner. Having learned what planners expect, the developer has submitted detailed specifications which he is confident will meet planning approval, and has bought land which already has outline planning permission. More recently, however, developers have acted somewhat more independently; for example, they have bought land which lacks detailed planning approval for development, but which lies in areas which are scheduled for development in the more general regional structure plans. If his proposals are rejected by local planners, the developer calculates that they have a strong likelihood of being approved by appeal to the Minister. The developer has increasingly come to play not merely the role of co-operator with the planning process, but also that of agitator against its constraints.

The developer's actions must also, of course, be set within more narrowly economic considerations, and, more particularly, within the context of the rapid rise in land prices which has meant that land costs now form a substantially greater proportion of the total selling price of houses (Drewett, 1973b). His reaction has been to build at higher density as well as to economize on construction costs by building many houses to lower standards. Not only does this mean that many of the cheaper range of private houses are now of a lower standard than many council houses, but that newer housing developments are often of higher density (both in the general density of layout and in their internal space standards) than much older housing. This helps partly to explain the otherwise surprising fact that the prices of old and new houses in many parts of the country differ very little (Thomas, 1973).

Despite the planning and economic constraints within which he operates, the developer can still be thought of as a partly independent agent in the housing market. Craven's (1969) work in Kent provides an effective example of this. He shows that the new large-scale developer needs large and relatively cheap areas of land if he is to exploit his potential scale-economies and provide cheap houses. Given the sharp fall in land values away from the centre of large towns such as Birmingham and London, the estates of relatively cheap, relatively low-density, standardized three-bedroom houses have been built by large developers in peripheral locations far removed from the centres of offic work in large towns. Medium-income families looking for housing withi their means have therefore been forced to move long distances from central London, whether they wished to or not. As Craven comments, rather than being a simple supplier of needs, the developer is an *indepe* *dent* actor 'who interprets, albeit inaccurately, major forces in the urba environment; an initiator of action based on this interpretation and a challenger of public policies which obstruct such action'.

Planners

It can be argued that the power of planners is largely illusory, that t] much-heralded 'teeth' of the planning machine are not very sharp. Buchanan's (1972) assessment of the contribution of twenty-five years of planning, for example, offers very subdued praise; he sees planners a having 'tidied-up' development, as having merely prevented worse thing from happening. The contributors to Hall's (1973) survey of urban dev opment likewise level charges of impotence at the planner; that he has failed, for instance, to control the rising price of land in the postwar period. Certainly, in a mixed economy the planner acts within the fram work of the logic of capital and is partly at the mercy of many aspects the free enterprise sector. This is nowhere better illustrated than in the redevelopment of central cities. By scheduling central land for commer cial development, planners have helped to create astronomical land pric in expectation of the potential profits from commercial building. Re-development has thus only been possible through private capital. In in-numerable towns, recent schemes of rebuilding have been undertaken ir conjunction with private companies; the planners compulsorily buying land, selling or leasing it to a developer, and approving his plans for offi development in return for the inclusion of a certain, and usually token, amount of housing or of public facilities. The developer has invariably made very handsome profits from the office development. London pro-vides many such instances, and a recent and dramatically large-scale example amongst provincial towns is that of Cardiff's central redevelop-ment scheme. Opponents of such schemes argue that they destroy exist-ing communities, rob central areas of their stock of cheap housing, and force workers to live ever further from their place of work. Local counc and planners, faced with high land prices (which their planning helps to create), argue that only by such means can their town centres be kept viab]

Nevertheless, despite working within a mixed and partly capitalist economy, the actions and the ideas of planners have had indisputable effects upon the shape of urban development and upon the nature of housing and housing estates. The containment of urban areas, which has a long history in the philosophy of British planning, has been one of the major conceptual planks and has had evident effects on urban development; while helping to preserve areas of non-urban land, it has also lengthened the 'journey-to-work'. The belief in medium- or low-density housing and in the separation of land uses, which derives from the Garden City movement at the turn of the century, again has had marked consequences, not least in the extra costs to which it has led. And such beliefs all too easily become institutionally fossilized into recommendations about the permitted widths of streets, the distances between houses, and traffic visibility at road intersections which planners have often applied with mindless rigidity.

Against the background of their belief in and execution of 'correct' principles of layout design, planners' ideas have also changed over time. One such change has been the move to higher levels of density which has left its mark in high-rise flats, the building of which has also been encouraged by the more generous subsidies given to development on expensive central land in towns. Such developments (certainly to judge by their adverse publicity and households' reluctance to move into them (Sutcliffe, 1974) may not represent what the customer most wants, and the fact that the housing system is partly bureaucratically controlled and partly open to free choice merely exacerbates any latent dissatisfaction at being forced to live in them. A further change of direction has been the move from redevelopment to rehabilitation (Kirwan and Martin, 1972), reflected in improvement grant legislation and in the designation of general improvement areas. The role of planners is now much less clear-cut than formerly, when the value of wholesale clearance of 'slum' areas was indisputable. Now that planners have developed the expertise and the machinery to effect the demolition and rebuilding of housing, they tend to use their juggernaut indiscriminately. And their actions are often 'justified' by the self-fulfilling prophecy of 'planner's blight' (Davies, 1972); once an area has been designated for clearance, that very designation helps to hasten the area's deterioration and so reinforces the apparent wisdom of clearance, even though the initial diagnosis may have been less than well-founded. Planners have been better geared to the relatively mechanical task of clearing houses than to the more sensitive job of accommodating social needs, and their attempts at involvement in community activity or in consultative exercises have not been notable successful (Dennis, 1972).

Planners, of course, are faced with an impossible brief: to bring certainty into a necessarily uncertain world, to accommodate and resolve the conflicting goals of many different individuals and land-users, to work for the public good in the context of a partly free-enterprise economy, to

reconcile social needs with individual ability to pay. Inevitably, from th
viewpoint of any individual, their effects have not always been benign,
nor even well advised. Certainly, one can argue that their impact has oft
been to increase rather than decrease the social polarity within urban so

In studying any town and its social areas, the problems and the polic
of actors such as these need very much to be borne in mind. As yet, geographers have not looked in great detail at the activities of land-owners
developers, planners, financiers, or at the effects of general legislation.
Such actions are, of course, very specific to a particular town, and their
study draws us away from the general urban models which geographers
have tried to develop. But in understanding the process of residential
development a more local focus is probably necessary. Legislation and
the logic of profit in our mixed economy provide a general backcloth,
but how they operate and how the individual actors fulfil their roles car
vary widely from one town to another. It is this variation which makes i
essential that geographers now look at individual towns: at how officials
within them interpret their roles, how they seek to resolve conflicting
interests, at how actors in the private sphere resolve the often competing
demands of private profit and the needs of the market for which they
cater. Why do some councils destroy older houses while others recognize
the scope for rehabilitation (Ministry of Housing and Local Government
1966)? How do developers 'read' market forces; do they cater more read
for immigrants to a town than for its existing households (Wyatt and
Winger, 1971)? What effects, in a local context, do specific pieces of
general legislation have? How do local councils' housing allocation polic
differ? We shall not be able to understand the nature of residential areas
unless we are able to answer these and similar questions about the processes by which towns develop. And we shall not be able to answer such
questions by looking at general models of urban structure. The constrai
within the housing market and the subdivisions within it suggest that it i
unrealistic to base all of our ideas upon the micro-economic assumption
that there is some equilibrium pattern towards which residential locatio
and urban land use move. If we are to understand the complex movemer
of households and the social areas which these moves produce, we need
to look at the economic and social contexts within which houses are bui
at the way in which local councils and planning bodies arrive at decision
at the actions of developers, financiers, speculators, and other actors, an
to trace the effects of general legislation on their actions. Only in such
ways can we begin to understand the process by which cities function
and residential areas emerge.

Further reading

There is a considerable literature which touches on aspects of urban social areas. The following suggestions are additions to those references already made in the text.

General surveys of urban geography include Carter (1972), Herbert (1972) and Johnston (1971). The writings of the Chicago ecologists are best represented in the reader by Theodorson (1961) and by Burgess and Bogue (1964). Factorial studies of towns are reviewed in Timms (1971) and Rees (1970); individual studies of British towns can be found in Gittus (1964), Robson (1969), Norman (1969), and Herbert (1970). Some examples of studies of the distribution of social phenomena include the following: on crime, mental disturbance, and ill-health, Bagley (1965), Morris (1957), Timms (1971), Galle *et al.* (1970), Griffiths (1971), Schorr (1964), Wilner *et al.* (1962); on education, Jackson and Marsden (1962), Robson (1969).

Buttimer (1969) discusses the differences between social and physical space very effectively. Harvey's (1973) stimulating social perspective on city structure introduces a radically fresh Marxist dialectical approach to urban social theory. The more traditional community studies conducted by sociologists are well summarized by Frankenberg (1966), who sees communities in terms of a rural/urban continuum— an amphasis which owes something to the classic essay by Wirth (1938) which embodied the ecologists' views of the effects of city life, but which has subsequently been heavily criticized both for the United States and for other countries (Berry, 1973). General discussion of urban sociological writings can be found in Pahl (1968 and 1970) and the collection of writings by Gans (1972) provides stimulating reading, arguing the merits of suburban life-styles and the limitations of placing too great an emphasis on environmental effects on social patterns. On this latter topic a very readable review is provided by Michelson (1970).

On the family life-cycle, early work which is well worth consulting includes Glick (1957), Leslie and Richardson (1961), and Lansing and Kish (1957). The connection with residential mobility is well explored by Simmons (1968), Speare (1970), and by Foote *et al.* (1960). An example of a British study of attitudes towards moving is Wilkinson (1965).

On housing, there is now a growing number of books on the early development of 'working class' housing (Tarn, 1973; Gauldie, 1974; Chapman, 1971), but for the recent period the writings of Cullingworth and Donnison are essential reading. Cullingworth's (1963) study of Lancaster draws upon some detailed information on property ownership in that town, and his more general work (1960, 1965, 1966) traces the connection between housing and public policy. Donnison (1967) provides a valuable comparison of housing in Britain, Europe, and America. Bowley (1945) looks at housing in the interwar period. The Milner Holland Report (Ministry of Housing and Local Government, 1965) contains details of conditions in London in the middle 1960s and discusses the problems of rented housing and its decline. More polemical views of housing in a capitalist economy can be found in the more fugitive literature of local community action groups, and an excellent example is the study of London provided by Counter Information Services (1973).

Studies of local authority housing in specific estates can be found in Jevons and Madge (1946), Williams (1939), and Ravetz (1974). More general works are Jennings (1971) and the Cullingworth report (Ministry of Housing and Local Government, 1969). The saga of the building of the Cutteslowe wall in Oxford (Collison, 1963) provides a dramatic symbol of the cleavage between private and council housing.

Housing statistics can be found in various of the H.M.S.O. publications of the Government Statistical Service (*Local Housing Statistics, Housing and Construction Statistics, Social Trends*) and in various issues of the *Occasional Bulletin* issued by the Nationwide Building Society. The Census is full of informative material.

There is little geographical work as yet on the role of individual actors in the housing market, but a most notable exception is the two-volume report of a P.E.P. study of urban development in England (Hall *et al.*, 1973). For the United States, Kaiser (1968) looks at aspects of individual builders. A most valuable study of the housing market in the London boroughs of Lambeth and Sutton was published after this book was written (Harloe *et al.*, 1974).

References

(Askerisks suggest references of general interest or of particular value)

*Abel-Smith, B. and Townsend, P. (1965) *The poor and the poorest*, Occasional Papers on Social Administration, **17** (Bell).

Abu-Lughod, J. (1969) 'Testing the theory of Social Area Analysis: the ecology of Cairo', *Am. Sociol. Rev.* **34**, 198–212.

Adams, J. S. (1969) 'Directional bias in intra-urban migration', *Econ. Geogr.* **45**, 303–23.

Alonso, W. (1964) *Location and land use* (Harvard U. P.).

Ambrose, P. (1974) *The quiet revolution: social change in a Sussex village 1871–1971* (Chatto and Windus)

Anderson, T. R. and Egeland, J. A. (1961) 'Spatial aspects of Social Area Analysis', *Am. Sociol. Rev.*, **26**, 392–8.

Bagley, C. (1965) 'Juvenile delinquency in Exeter: an ecological and comparative study', *Urban Stud.*, **2**, 33–50.

Barbolet, R. H. (1969) 'Housing classes and the socio-ecological system', *Univ. Working Paper*, **4**, Centre of Environmental Studies, London.

Barnett, A. S., *et al.* (1970) 'Some factors underlying racial discrimination in housing: a preliminary report on Manchester', *Race*, **12**, 75–85.

Beresford, M. W. (1971) 'The back-to-back house in Leeds, 1787–1937', *in* Chapman S. D. (ed.) op. cit., 93–132.

Berry, B. J. L. (1965) 'Internal structure of the city', *Law and Contemporary Problems*, **30**, 111–19.

*– (1973) *The human consequences of urbanisation* (Macmillan).

*Beshers, J. M. (1962) *Urban social structure* (Free Press)

– and Laumann, E. O. (1967) 'Social distance: a network approach', *Am. Sociol. Rev.* **32**, 225–36.

Boal, F. W. (1969) 'Territoriality on the Shankhill-Falls divide, Belfast', *Irish Geogr.* **6**, 30–60.

– (1972) 'The urban residential sub-community: a conflict interpretations', *Area*, **4**, 164–8.

Bowley, M. E. A. (1945) *Housing and the State, 1919–44* (Allen and Unwin).

Brown, L. A. and Holmes, J. (1971) 'Search behaviour in an intra-urban migration context: a spatial perspective', *Envir. Plann.* **3**, 307–26.

* –and Moore, E. G. (1970) 'The intra-urban migration process: a perspective', *Geogr Annaler*, **52B**, 1–13.

Buchanan, C. (1972) *The state of Britain* (Faber).

Bullock, N., *et al.* (1972) 'The modelling of day to day activities', *in* Martin, L. and March, L. (eds.) *Urban space and structures* (Cambridge U. P.), 129–57.

Burgess, E. W. and Bogue, D. J. (eds.) (1964) *Contributions to urban sociology* (U. Chicago P.).

Burney, E. (1967) *Housing on trial* (Oxford U. P.).

*Buttimer, A. (1969) 'Social space in interdisciplinary perspective', *Geogrl Rev.* **59** 417–26.

Carter, H. (1970) 'A decision-making approach to town plan analysis', *in* Carter, H. and Davies, W. K. D. (eds.) *Urban essays* (Longman) 66–78.

*–(1972) *The study of urban geography* (Arnold).

Casetti, E. (1967) 'Urban population density patterns: an alternate explanation', *Canadian Geogr.*, **11**, 96–101.

Chapin, F. S., Jr. (1965) *Urban land use planning* (U. Illinois P.). 2nd Edn.

– (1968) 'Activity systems and urban structure: a working schema', *J. Am. Inst. Planners*, **34**, 11–18.

Chapman, S. D. (ed.) (1971) *The history of working-class housing* (David and Charles).

Clawson, M. and Hall, P. (1973) *Planning and urban growth: an Anglo-American comparison* (Johns Hopkins U. P.).

Coates, K. and Silburn, R. (1970) *Poverty: the forgotten Englishmen* (Penguin).

Collison, P. (1963) *The Cutteslowe walls: a study in social class* (Faber).

–and Mogey, J. M. (1959) 'Residence and social class in Oxford', *Am. J. Sociol.*, **64**, 599–605.

*Counter Information Services (1973) *The recurrent crisis of London: anti-report on property developers*, London, 2nd edn.

Cox, K. R. (1973) *Conflict, power and politics in the city: a geographic view* (McGraw-Hill).

*Craven, E. A. (1969) 'Private residential expansion in Kent', *Urban Stud.,* 6, 1—16.

Cullingworth, J. B. (1960) *Housing needs and planning policy* (R. & K. P.).

*— (1963) *Housing in transition: a case study in the city of Lancaster* (R. & K. P.).

— (1965) *English housing trends: a report on the Rowntree Trust Housing Study,* Occasional Papers on Social Administration, 13,(Bell).

*— (1966) *Housing and local government in England and Wales* (Allen and Unwin).

Dalton, M. and Seaman, J. M. (1973) 'The distribution of New Commonwealth immigrants in the London borough of Ealing, 1961—66' *Trans. Inst. Br. Geogr.,* 58, 21—39.

*Davies, J. Gower (1972) *The evangelistic bureaucrat* (Tavistock).

Deakin, N. and Cohen, B. G. (1970) 'Dispersal and choice: towards a strategy for ethic minorities in Britain', *Envir. Plann:* 2, 193—201.

Dennis, N. (1958) 'The popularity of the neighbourhood community idea', *Sociol. Rev.,* 6, 191—206.

*— (1970) *People and planning* (Faber).

— (1972) *Public participation and planners' blight* (Faber).

Donnison, D. V. (1961) 'The movement of households in England', *Jl. R. Statist. Soc.,* 124A, 60—80.

*—(1967) *The government of housing* (Penguin).

Douglas J. W. B. (1964) *The home and the school* (MacGibbon and Kee).

*Drewett, R. (1973a) 'The developers: decision processes', *in* Hall, P. *et. al.* op. cit., vol. 2, pp. 163—93.

*— (1973b) 'Land values and the suburban land market', *in* Hall, P. *et al.* op. cit., vol. 2, pp. 197—245.

*Duncan, O. D. and Duncan, B. (1955) 'Residential distribution and occupational stratification', *Am. J. Sociol.,* 60, 493—506.

Duncan, S. S. (1974) 'Cosmetic planning or social engineering: improvement grants and improvement areas in Hull', *Area,* 6.

Durant, R. (1939) *Watling: a survey of social life on a new housing estate* (P. S. King).

Dyos, H. J. and Reeder, D. A. (1973) 'Slums and suburbs', *in* Dyos, H. J. and Wolf, M., (eds.) *The Victorian city* (R. & K. P.), 359—86.

Evans, A. W. (1973) *The economics of residential location* (Macmillan).

Festinger, L., Schachter, S., and Back, K. W. (1950) *Social pressures in informal groups: a study of human factors in housing* (Harper).

Fisher, E. M. and Winnick, L. (1951) 'A reformulation of the filtering concept', *J. Social Issues,* 7, 47—58.

*Foote, N. N., Abu-Lughod, J., Foley, M. M., and Winnick, L. (1960) *Housing choices and housing constraints* (McGraw-Hill).

*Frankenberg, R. (1966) *Communities in Britain* (Penguin).

Fried, M. and Gleicher, P. (1961) 'Some sources of residential satisfaction in an urban slum', *J. Am. Inst. Planners,* 27, 305—15.

Fuerst, J. S. (ed.) (1974) *Public housing in Europe and America* (Croom Helm).

Galle, O. R. *et al.* (1970) 'Population density and pathology: what are the relations for man?' *Science,* 176, 23—30.

*Gans, H. J. (1972) *People and plans* (Penguin), abridged edn.

Gauldie, E. (1974) *Cruel habitations* (Allen and Unwin) .

Giggs, J. A. (1970) 'Socially disorganised areas in Barry' *in* Carter, H. and Davies, W. K. D. (eds.) *Urban essays* (Longman), 101—43.

— (1973) 'The distribution of schizophrenics in Nottingham', *Trans. Inst. Br. Geogr.,* 59, 55—76.

Gittus, E. (1964) 'An experiment in the definition of urban sub-areas', *Trans. Bartlett Soc.,* 2, 109—35.

Glass, R. (1970) 'Housing in Camden', *Town Planning Rev.,* 41, 15—40.

Glick, P. (1957) *American families* (Wiley).

Goldthorpe, J. H., Lockwood, D., *et al.* (1969) *The affluent worker in the class structure* (Cambridge U. P.).

Gould, P. R. and White, R. (1974) *Mental maps* (Penguin).

*Gracey, H. (1973) 'The planners: control of new residential development', *in* Hall, P. *et al.* op. cit., vol. 2, pp. 126—45.

Gray, F. G. (1974) Personal communication (from work on vacancy chains, the topic of his postgraduate work at Cambridge University).

Grayler, H. J. (1970) 'Land speculation and urban development: contrasts in south-east Essex, 1880–1940', *Urban Stud.*, 7, 21–36.

Griffiths, M. (1971) 'A geographical study of mortality in an urban area', *Urban Stud.*, 8, 111–20.

Grigsby, W. G. (1963) *Housing markets and public policy* (U. Pennsylvania P.).

Haddon, R. F. (1970) 'A minority in a welfare state society', *The New Atlantis*, 2, 80–133.

Hagerstrand, T. (1969) 'What about people in regional science?' *Papers and Proceedings, Reg. Sci. Ass.*, 24, 7–21.

*Hall, P. *et al.* (1973) *The containment of urban England* (Allen and Unwin), 2 v

Hamnett, C. (1973) 'Improvement grants as an indicator of gentrification in Inner London', *Area*, 5, 252–61.

Harloe, M. *et al.* (1974) *The organization of housing: public and private enterprise in London* (Heinemann).

*Harvey, D. (1973) *Social justice and the city* (Arnold).

Heraud, B. J. (1968) 'Social class and the New Towns', *Urban Stud.* 5, 33–58.

Herbert, D. T. (1970) 'Principal components analysis and urban social structure: a study of Cardiff and Swansea', *in* Carter, H. and Davies, W. K. D. (eds.) *Urban essays* (Longman), 97–100.

*– (1972) *Urban geography: a social perspective* (David and Charles).

– (1973) 'The residential mobility process: some empirical observations', *Area*, 5, 44–8.

Hillery, G. A. Jr. (1955) 'Definitions of community: areas of agreement', *Rural Sociol.*, 20, 111–23.

Holmes, R. S. (1973) 'Ownership and migration from a study of rate books', *Area*, 5, 242–51.

Hoyt, H. (1939) *The structure and growth of residential neighbourhoods in American cities* (Federal Housing Administration).

Jackson, B. and Marsden, D. (1962) *Education and the working class* (R. & K. P.).

Jackson, J. A. (1963) *The Irish in Britain* (R. & K. P.).

*Jennings, J. H. (1971) 'Geographical implications of the municipal housing programme in England and Wales', *Urban Stud.*, 8, 121–38.

Jevons, R. and Madge, J. (1946) *Housing estates* (Arrowsmith).

Johnston, R. J. (1971) *Urban residential patterns* (Bell).

*Jones, E. (1960) *A social geography of Belfast* (Oxford U. P.).

Jones, P. N. (1970) 'Some aspects of the changing distribution of coloured immigrants in Birmingham, 1961–66', *Trans. Inst. Br. Geogr.*, 50, 199–219.

Kain, J. F. and Quigley, J. M. (1970) 'Evaluating the quality of the residential environment', *Envir. Plann.*, 2, 23–32.

Kaiser, E. J. (1968) 'Locational decision factors in a producer model of residential development', *Land Econ.*, 44, 351–62.

Karn, V. (1969) 'Property values amongst Indians and Pakistanis in a Yorkshire town', *Race*, 10, 69–83.

Kellett, J. R. (1969) *The impact of railways on Victorian cities* (R. & K. P.).

Kirkby, D. A. (1971) 'The interwar council dwelling: a study of residential obsolescence and decay', *Town Plann. Rev.*, 42, 250–68.

Kirwan, R. M. and Martin, D. B. (1971) 'Some notes on housing market models for urban planning', *Envir. Plann.*, 3, 243–52.

– and Martin, D. B. (1972) 'The economics of urban residential renewal and improvement', *Working Paper*, 77, Centre of Environmental Studies, London

Kuper, L. (1953) 'Blueprint for living together', *in* Kuper, L. *et al.* (eds.) *Living in towns* (Cresset Press).

Landay, S. (1971) 'The ecology of Islamic cities: the case for the ethnocity', *Econ. Geogr.*, 47 (Supplement), 303–13.

*Lansing, J. B. *et al.* (1969) *New homes and poor people: a study of chains of moves* (Inst. for Social Research, Univ. of Michigan).

– and Kish, L. (1957) 'Family life cycle as an independent variable', *Am. Sociol. Rev.*, 22, 512–19.

Lave, L. B. (1970) 'Congestion and urban location', *Papers and Proceedings, Reg. Sci. Ass.*, 25, 133–50.

Lee, T. R. (1973) 'Ethnic and social class factors in residential segregation: some implications for dispersal', *Envir. Plann.*, 5, 477–90.

Leslie, G. R. and Richardson, A. H.(1961) 'Life cycle, career pattern and the decision to move', *Am. Sociol. Rev.*, 26, 894–902.

Lowry, I. (1960) 'Filtering and housing standards', *Land Econ.* 36, 362–70.

Lynch, K. (1960) *The image of the city* (M. I. T. Press).

Mellor, R. (1973) 'Structure and process in the twilight areas', *Town Plann. Rev.*, 44, 54–70.

Michelson, W. (1970) *Man and his urban environment* (Addison-Wesley).

Ministry of Housing and Local Government (1965) *Report of the Committee on Housing in Greater London* (Milner Holland Report) (H.M.S.O.)

– (1966) *The Deeplish study* (H.M.S.O.).

– (1969) *Council housing* (Cullingworth Report) (H.M.S.O.).

Mitchell, B. R. (1962) *Abstract of British historical statistics* (Cambridge U. P.).

Mogey, J. M. (1956) *Family and neighbourhood* (Oxford U. P.).

Morris, R. N. and Mogey, J. M. (1965) *The sociology of housing* (R. & K. P.).

Morris, T. (1957) *The criminal area* (R. & K. P.).

Mortimore, M. J. (1969) 'Landownership and urban growth in Bradford and its environs in the West Riding conurbation', *Trans. Inst. Br. Geogr.*, 46, 99–113.

Moser, C. A. and Scott, W. (1961) *British towns* (Oliver and Boyd).

Musgrove, F. (1963) *The migratory elite* (Heinemann).

Musil, J. (1968) 'The development of Prague's ecological structure', *in* Pahl, R. E. (ed.) *Readings in urban sociology* (Pergamon), 232–59.

Muth, R. F. (1969) *Cities and housing* (U. Chicago P.).

Nationwide Building Society (1970) 'Why do people move?', *Occasional Bulletin*, 99.

Nevitt, A. A. (1966) *Housing, taxation and subsidies* (Nelson).

Norman, P. (1969) 'Third survey of London life and labour', *in* Dogan, M. and Rokkan, S. (eds.) *Quantitative ecological analysis in the social sciences* (M.I.T. Press), 371–96.

Olsen, D. J. (1973) 'House upon house: estate development in London and Sheffield', *in* Dyos, H. J. and Wolf, M. (eds.) *The Victorian city* (R. & K. P.), 333–57.

Pahl, R. E. (1968) 'A perspective on urban sociology', *in* Pahl, R. E. (ed.) *Readings in urban sociology* (Pergamon), 3–44.

– (1970) *Patterns of urban life* (Longman).

– (1971) 'Poverty and the urban system', *in* Chisholm, M. and Manners, G. (eds.) *Spatial policy problems of the British economy* (Cambridge U. P.), 126–45.

Park, R. E., Burgess, E. W., and McKenzie, R. D. (1925) *The city* (U. Chicago P.), reprinted 1967.

Peterson, G. L. (1967) 'A model of preference: quantitative analysis of the perception of the visual appearance of residential neighbourhoods', *J. Reg. Sci.*, 7, 19–31.

Poole, M. A. and Boal, F. W. (1973) 'Religious segregation in Belfast in mid-1969: a multi-level analysis', *in* Institute of British Geographers, *Special Publication*, No. 5 (Social patterns in cities), 1–40.

Pritchard, R. M. (1972) 'Intra-urban migration in Leicester, 1860–1965', Unpublished Ph.D. thesis, Univ. of Cambridge.

Ramsøy, N. R. (1966) 'Assortive mating and the structure of cities', *Am. Sociol. Rev.*, 31, 773–86.

Ratcliffe, R. U. (1949) *Urban land economics* (McGraw-Hill).

Ravetz, A. (1974) *Model estate: planned housing at Quarry Hill, Leeds* (Croom Helm).

Rees, P. H. (1970) 'Concepts of social space: toward an urban social geography', *in* Berry, B. J. L. and Horton, F. E. (eds.) *Geographic perspectives on urban systems* (Prentice-Hall), 306–94.

Rex, J. (1968) 'The sociology of a zone in transition', *in* Pahl, R. E. (ed.) *Readings in urban sociology* (Pergamon), 211–31.

– and Moore, R. (1967) *Race community and conflict* (Oxford U. P.).

Richardson, C. (1968) 'Irish settlement in mid-nineteenth century Bradford', *Yorks. Bull. Econ. Soc. Res.* 20, 40–57.

Robinson, W. S. (1950) 'Ecological correlations and the behaviour of individuals', *Am. Sociol. Rev.*, 15, 351–7.

Robson, B. T. (1969) *Urban analysis:* (Cambridge U. P.).
*− (1973) 'A view on the urban scene', *in* Chisholm, M. and Rodgers, B. (eds.) *Studies in human geography* (Heinemann), 203−41.
Rose, E. J. B. (1969) *Colour and citizenship* (Oxford U. P.).
*Rossi, P. H. (1955) *Why families move* (Free Press).
*Runciman, W. G. (1966) *Relative deprivation and social justice* (R. & K. P.).
*Schorr, A. L. (1964) *Slums and social insecurity* (Nelson).
Shevky, E. and Bell, W. (1955) *Social Area Analysis:* (Stanford U. P.).
*Simmons, J. W. (1968) 'Changing residence in the city', *Geogrl Rev.*, 58, 622−51.
Speare, A. (1970) 'Home ownership, life cycle stage and residential mobility', *Demography*, 7, 449−58.
Stacey, M. (1960) *Tradition and change* (Oxford U. P.).
Sutcliffe, A. (ed.) (1974) *Multi-storey living* (Croom Helm).
*Sweetser, F. L. (1969) 'Ecological factors in metropolitan zones and sectors', *in* Dogan, M. and Rokkan, S. (eds.) *Quantitative ecological analysis in the social sciences* (M.I.T. Press), 413−56.
Tarn, J. N. (1973) *Five per cent philanthropy: an account of housing in urban area between 1840 and 1914* (Cambridge U. P.).
*Theodorson, G. A. (ed.) (1961) *Studies in human ecology* (Row, Peterson).
*Thomas, R. (1973) 'Housing trends and urban growth', *in* Hall, P. *et al.* op. cit., vol. 2, pp. 246−94.
*Timms, D. W. G. (1971) *The urban mosaic* (Cambridge U. P.).
Tucker, J. (1966) *Honourable estates* (Gollancz).
Ward, D. (1962) 'The pre-urban cadaster and the urban pattern of Leeds', *Ann. Ass. Am. Geogr.*, 52, 150−66.
Watson, C. J. (1973) 'Household movement in West Central Scotland: a study of housing chains and filtering', *Occasional Paper*, 26, Centre for Urban and Regional Studies, Univ. of Birmingham.
Webber, M. M. (1963) 'Order in diversity: community without propinquity', *in* Wingo, L. Jr. (ed.) *Cities and space* (Johns Hopkins U. P.), 23−54.
− (1964) 'The urban place and the nonplace urban realm', *in* Webber, M. M. *et al.* (eds.) *Explorations into urban structure* (U. Pennsylvania P.), 79−153.
Westergaard, J. H. (1964) 'The structure of Greater London', *in* Centre for Urban Studies, *London: aspects of change* (MacGibbon and Kee), 91−144.
Whitbread, M. and Bird, H. (1973) 'Rent, surplus and the evaluation of residential environments', *Reg. Stud.*, 7, 193−223.
White, H. C. (1971) 'Multipliers, vacancy chains and filtering in housing', *J. Am. Inst. Planners*, 37, 88−94.
Whyte, W. F. (1943) *Street corner society* (U. Chicago P.).
Wilkinson, R. (1965) 'A statistical analysis of attitudes to moving (a survey of slum clearance areas in Leeds)', *Urban Stud.*, 2, 1−14.
Williams, N. (1939) *Population problems of new estates* (U. Liverpool P.).
Willmott, P. (1963) *The evolution of a community* (R. & K. P.).
− and Young, M. (1960) *Family and class in a London suburb* (R. & K. P.).
Wilner, D. M., Walkley, R. P., *et al.* (1962) *The housing environment and family life* (Johns Hopkins U. P.).
Winnick, L. (1966) 'Development values and controls', *in* Senior, D. (ed.) *The regional city* (Longman), 125−33.
Wirth, L. (1938) 'Urbanism as a way of life', *Am. J. Sociol.*, 44, 1−24.
Wyatt, G. L. and Winger, A. R. (1971) 'Residential construction, mover origin and urban form', *Reg. Stud.*, 5, 95−9.
Young, M. and Willmott, P. (1957) *Family and kinship in East London* (R. & K. P.).
−− (1973) *The symmetrical family* (R. & K. P.).